Jesus
still has something to say

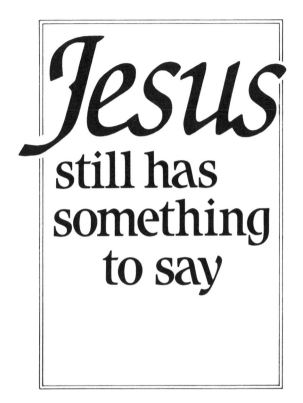

Jesus still has something to say

Robert C. Campbell

Judson Press ® Valley Forge

JESUS STILL HAS SOMETHING TO SAY

Copyright © 1987
Judson Press, Valley Forge, PA 19482-0851

Unless otherwise indicated, Bible quotations in this volume are from the Revised Standard Version of the Bible, copyrighted 1946, 1952(c), 1971, 1973 by the Division of Christian Education of the National Council of the Churches of Christ in the U.S.A., and used by permission.

Other versions of the Bible quoted in this book are:
The Holy Bible, King James Version.
The New Testament in Modern English, rev. ed. Copyright © J. B. Phillips 1972. Used by permission of The Macmillan Company and Geoffrey Bles, Ltd.

Library of Congress Cataloging-in-Publication Data

Campbell, Robert C.
  Jesus still has something to say.

  1. Jesus Christ—Teachings.   2. Christian Life—
Biblical teaching.   I. Title.
BS2417.C5C36   1987   230   87-4169
ISBN 0-8170-1114-5

Jesus
still has
something
to say

Acknowledgments

I offer thanks to all who contributed to this work:

—to the many scholars, colleagues, and friends whose thoughts are here contained;

—to Lotus, my wife, who encourages me in every endeavor;

—to Isabelle Cahill, my secretary, whose extended and able labors are reflected throughout;

—to Laura Alden of Judson Press for her constructive criticism and helpful suggestions; and

—to the Executive Committee of the General Board of the American Baptist Churches in the U.S.A., who made time available by encouraging me to take a break from my regular responsibilities.

All these and many unmentioned share in any ministry of this work, but I alone am accountable for its shortcomings.

Robert C. Campbell
Valley Forge, Pa.
September 1986

Contents

Preface

This volume is offered as a bridge between biblical scholarship and the Christian leader who seeks spiritual insight and enrichment rooted in Scripture. In pursuing this purpose, it represents a level of scholarly study, including appropriate textual, literary, and historical homework. It also attempts a communicable idiom with appropriate illustration.

A wealth of technical material is available to ministers and interested laity. But in the main it is tough reading. On the other hand, there is no want of devotional literature coming off the presses. Beyond that, books of sermons abound. This work is none of these. It is Bible study centered on crucial questions related to Christian life. It is rooted in scholarship but conducted with inobtrusive technical tools. It is devotional in purpose but calls for a commitment of mind. It borders on preaching but needs transposition to one's own experience.

In 1763 Indian tribes responded to white brutality with massacres. John Woolman, against the prudent advice of friends, determined to speak to Chief Papunahung. He spoke through interpreters, but the message was not getting through. Finally Woolman, in frustration, prayed aloud with great emotion and gesticulation in English. The chief, while not understanding a word, said, "I love to feel where words come from!"[1]

I want the reader to both see and feel where these words come from. Effective communication is more concrete than abstract; hence the illustrative material. Christian response also involves emotion. The Word calls for involvement, growth, and change.

This work tries to express that call. In attempting to combine devotional, evangelistic, and scholarly concerns, it is intended and offered as a ministry. It is my earnest hope to encourage and enrich ministers of the gospel and concerned Christian laity. Jesus still has something to say to all of us.

Jesus
still has something to say

Chapter One

Who Are We—
Angels or Devils?

The Teachings of Jesus Concerning Human Nature

D oes listening to news broadcasts make you reflect on how much bad there is in so many of us? It is obvious that much of what constitutes our news reflects violence, hatred, human exploitation, and conflict. Indeed, there is so much negative news that it can cause us to despair. This phenomenon has led Doug Larson to observe: "Children like to listen to scary stories before bedtime. Adults watch the late news."

It is not only radio and television that reflect the wrongs of our nature and human predicament. Take the front page of any metropolitan newspaper. Then cut out every article that shows something wrong with us as people or expresses how we don't get along together. This means that all the war news, crimes, strikes, oppression—indeed, all illegal activities and human disagreements—will be cut out. Then see how much of a front page is left!

Thus Robert Orben wonders what has happened to the good news. "Nowadays," he says, "you pick up the morning paper and right away you're 'filled to the brim'—with grim."

But occasionally there appears an oasis of encouragement in this desert of disagreement. It is that human interest article about one life risked to save another or about a sacrificial gift to a needy cause or individual. Note, for example, the international coverage of the dedicated service of Mother Teresa and her Sisters of Charity:

> The sight of this five foot nun ministering to the dying moved city
> officials to give her a *dharmsala* (inn) opposite Calcutta's famous
> Temple of Kali, the Hindu goddess of death. But many Brahmins
> objected to having a Christian center so near a Hindu holy place and
> stoned the windows, demanding her removal. One morning Mother
> Teresa picked up a man dying of cholera outside the temple and
> looked after him until death. The man was a temple priest, and her
> compassion so moved another Hindu holy man that he knelt before
> her and said: "For thirty years I have served the goddess Kali in her
> temple. Now the goddess stands before me."[1]

Such articles are the exception rather than the rule. Nevertheless, they lead us to realize that we are not all bad all the time.

'Specks' and 'Logs'

It is precisely at this point that we must beware. We instinctively
identify with Mother Teresa or other unselfish persons. Even children feel they belong with the "good guys" in movie or television
presentations. Thus we take the next step of making others the villains. Instead of evaluating others honestly—much less caring for
them—we criticize and judge. It is easier for us to see the wrongs of
others than to see our own.

In fact, we are likely to project our own failings as we sense them
in another person. G.B. White described the process well:

> I am neat and orderly; you are a little officious; he is a fussbudget.
> My dog is outgoing and friendly; yours is a public nuisance; theirs
> will hear from my lawyer. I don't intend to kill myself working; you
> are a little slack; he is a deadbeat. I had a disagreement with the IRS;
> you used some questionable deduction; he was busted by the Feds.

Jesus was more serious and more piercing in his observation:

> "Why do you see the speck that is in your brother's eye, but do not
> notice the log that is in your own eye? Or how can you say to your
> brother, 'Let me take the speck out of your eye,' when there is a log in
> your own eye? You hypocrite, first take the log out of your own eye,
> and then you will see clearly to take the speck out of your brother's
> eye" (Matthew 7:3–5).

We must take care to evaluate both ourselves and others objec-
tively.

This discussion brings us to the question, "Who are we—angels or devils?" The message of Jesus is that we are invested as God's creatures with dignity and incalculable value.

On the other hand, Jesus describes us as alienated from God and one another, failing—and even refusing—to achieve the potential with which God has invested us. In short, we are lost.

Jesus teaches that our origin is divine and our direction demonic. This tension is explicated throughout the Scriptures and is reflected in experience.

The Bible poses the question of our identity and answers that question in various ways. Note Psalm 8, for example: "When I consider thy heavens, the work of thy fingers, the moon and the stars, which thou hast ordained; What is man, that thou art mindful of him?" (Psalm 8:3–4 KJV).[2]

Have you been away from the lights of the cities—on the desert, in the mountains, or out at sea—and looked up to see how bright the stars are and how large and close they seem to be? It is difficult to conceive how anyone can claim to be an atheist at such a time. Such was the experience of Abraham Lincoln:

> Someone came running up the steps, and pounded sharply on the door. Abraham admitted a young man. "Mr. Lincoln, old lady Westly is dying. She sent me to ask you to come write her will."
>
> Abraham turned to Mary. "Would you keep me company?"
>
> It was an hour's ride in the cold autumnal night, the fields lying in dark stubble. When they reached the farmhouse Abraham asked Mrs. Westly a few simple questions, and wrote the will. She asked in a feeble voice if he would read from the Bible. One of the woman's sons offered him their copy, but he shook his head, reciting from the twenty-third Psalm: " 'though I walk through the valley of the shadow of death, I will fear no evil; for thou art with me. . . .' " As they were riding home in the predawn darkness, sitting close under the blanket, Mary said, "Pastor Lincoln, you did real well for a man who is not supposed to have a religion."
>
> Abraham looked up. The heavens were full of stars. He called off a few of their names.
>
> "I can see how it might be possible for a man to look down upon the earth and be an atheist, but I cannot conceive how he could look up into the heavens and say there is no God."
>
> They rode in silence for another moment, then she felt his hand reach out and take hers.[3]

The Crown of God

Experiences of meditation under the heavens also underscore our finitude. We feel small and insignificant. Thus we expect the psalmist to say that we are nothing but mere creatures on this one speck of cosmic dust while God relates to all of the celestial bodies in space. The surprising biblical answer emphasizes our importance.

> For thou hast made him a little lower than the angels, and hast crowned him with glory and honour. Thou madest him to have dominion over the works of thy hands; thou hast put all *things* under his feet . . ." (Psalm 8:5–6 KJV).

In short, we have great dignity!

Such understanding of dignity and self–acceptance leads us to accept others, to seek for God's gracious shalom. Kurt Vonnegut expressed this motivation well when he addressed a graduating class at Bennington College:

> I beg you to believe in the most ridiculous superstition of all: that humanity is at the center of the universe, the fulfiller or frustrater of the grandest dreams of God Almighty. If you can believe that, and make others believe it, human beings might stop treating each other like garbage.

This concept of humanity as limited and insignificant but at the same time possessing great God–given dignity is reflected throughout the Scriptures. On the one hand, God is pictured as forming us out of the dust of the ground. This scene obviously points to our limitation, our relation to this world, our connection with the animals which were also made from earth. On the other hand, God created us in the divine image and gave us dominion over all other living creatures. Throughout the Old Testament humanity is shown as humble in origin (from the earth). This picture is provided so that we might recognize our limitation and in turn stand in humble relationship before God. But we were also given the earth to exercise stewardship over it and rule the whole of nature, limited only by the command and will of God.

Our conquest of the natural realm through the technological advances of our day is not condemned by the Bible. Indeed, the Bible calls us to care for and properly use our natural resources as

God's creation. Sydney J. Harris speaks prophetically in his challenge that we not give in to selfishness because the world is sometimes a jungle. "It can also be a garden," says Harris, "depending on whether one wants to plant and water, or to plunder and uproot."

The Bible charges us to care for both the creation and creatures of God. We are responsible to relate ecologically to what God has made and to relate justly—even lovingly—with those created in the image of God. Professor Charles Birch made this point in addressing the Fifth Assembly of the World Council of Churches in Nairobi. He connected human justice and the renewal of the earth and human injustice and environmental deterioration. Using the example of the industrialist who contaminates the air and the youth who vandalizes a railway carriage, Birch maintained that "when people no longer care about people, they no longer care about the world."[4]

We fall under the judgment of the Bible when we fail to relate with one another or with God and creation. Strange, isn't it, how we seem to control everything around us while we cannot handle ourselves? This led the apostle Paul to "see in my members another law at war with the law of my mind and making me captive to the law of sin which dwells in my members" (Romans 7:23).

Johann Wolfgang von Goethe said that it was regrettable that nature had made only one of him, since there was enough material within him for at least two people—a rogue and a gentleman. An African pastor put it less elegantly in describing himself as having two dogs within, one a kindly pet and the other a vicious attacker. When asked which dog wins the inner battle, he responded, "It depends on which one I feed."

Part of the background of Jesus' statements about what we are is the biblical teaching that we are both dignified and demonic—at once God-like and devilish. This twofold view of human nature was also presented by the pagan teachers of Jesus' day. One of the greatest of these teachers was Seneca, a stoic philosopher and the personal teacher of Emperor Nero. By human standards Seneca was a good man but he spoke of himself as a man who could not be tolerated. On the other hand, he said, "God is near you, with you, within you . . . a holy spirit sits within us . . . our guardian." What if we had approached some of the nonbiblical writers of Jesus' day?

How would they have answered the question: "Who are we—angels or devils?" Their answer, likely, would be "neither or both." We seem to be angelic at some points and demonic at others. Indeed, Seneca also said that people love and hate their vices all at the same time. So the early philosophers agreed with the biblical writers. We are both good and bad.

Letting the Children Come

Let's examine our Lord's teaching more closely. As we have noted, one of the great emphases of Jesus is human dignity. We are created by God and are developing our potential under God.

Jesus differs from the philosophic teachers in method. He does not define essential human nature; our peculiar relationship with God and the universe; the distinctive elements in a human being such as body, soul or spirit; nor what constitutes that mysterious something we call personality. His teaching is not, basically, psychological or philosophical. It goes deeper. Jesus describes our divine origin and God's love for us and models the way we should accept ourselves—based on our value and significance.

The value that Jesus places upon us and the dignity with which he invests us are reflected in several Gospel accounts: spoke about children. We read, for example, that

> . . . they were bringing children to him . . . and the disciples rebuked them. But when Jesus saw it he was indignant, and said to them, "Let the children come to me, do not hinder them; for to such belongs the kingdom of God. Truly, I say to you, whoever does not receive the kingdom of God like a child shall not enter it" (Matthew 10:13-15).

Jesus observed that children (far better than adults) reflect what God is like and what we should be like. It is only as we take on that simplicity and honesty of expression, that receptivity and humble acceptance of our belonging—as children do—that we can receive the kingdom of God. The child seems to be more truly human than any of us. The child has not learned to cover up deep feelings with contemporary sophistication. Openness, honesty, true humanity—these are the elements beloved of God.

Jesus' view of our worth and dignity is also reflected in his comparison of our value as greater than that of the natural world, particularly than that of the animal kingdom. But this comparison does not mean that he despised animals. Rather, his attitude was expressed by Francis of Assisi, famed for his depth of devotion to the creatures that surrounded him. Legends have Francis preaching to these "brothers and sisters who flitted from one tree to another and who sat on the branches to hear his gospel proclamation." Just birds, we would say. But not for Francis! Nor for Francis' Lord. Not a single sparrow falls to the ground without the knowledge of God, Jesus said. And when he described the lost sheep, it was not just a matter of the shepherd going out to find it. He reflected, rather, his own concern—and that of God's—by saying that "when he has found it, he lays it on his shoulders, rejoicing" (Luke 15:5).

This theme reflects not so much Jesus' concern for the animal world as it does his estimate of our value. When those who were criticizing his work asked him about healing a needy person on the sabbath day, he emphasized the superiority of humans:
mals by saying:

> ". . . What man of you, if he has one sheep and it falls into a pit on the sabbath, will not lay hold of it and lift it out? Of how much more value is a man than a sheep! So it is lawful to do good on the sabbath" (Matthew 12:11–12).

Our value is greater than that of any other creature.

We can probably best understand the premium placed upon us in the teaching of our Lord not in his comparison of the adult with the child nor of the human being with the animal but in his expectations of us as persons. The demands Jesus makes in terms of our relationship with God could only be made to those in whom he sees great potential and value.

Pointing to Our Potential

Jesus underscores our potential:
"You are the salt of the earth. . . .
"You are the light of the world. . . .
"Love your enemies. . . .
"Seek first the kingdom of God. . . .
"Judge not."

Jesus goes so far in his assumption of our ability to respond to God that he demands of us, "You, therefore, must be perfect, as your heavenly Father is perfect" (Matthew 5:48). He does not call for moral perfection. Neither the context nor the Greek word reflects such absolutism. We are, rather, to be mature in our dealings with people as is God who "sends rain on the just and on the unjust" (Matthew 5:45). The fact that Jesus can demand the type of maturity and love of others that God manifests toward us reflects the potential Jesus assumes we possess.

There is also the other side of the coin. Jesus' view of humanity is extremely realistic. He saw that we are out of joint, disconnected, unrelated. We were made by God in order to live in relationship—with ourselves, with other persons, and with God. When we "come to ourselves" (Luke 15:17) we are prepared to relate. When we properly relate to others we fulfill our potential and become truly human. We cannot "go it" alone. Above all, we need to relate with God who is the basis and purpose of our life in the world.

Jesus recognized that we are not related properly at any one of these levels. On the contrary, we are estranged from our true selves, our neighbors, and our God. This estrangement and rebellion are what the Bible calls sin. Sin is failure to fulfill potential. It is failure to be what we should be, what we were made by God to be, and what we really want to be down deep.

This biblical perception of sin is presented whimsically in "Peanuts" as Linus observes:

> "Hands are fascinating things! I like my hands. . . . I think I have nice hands. . . . My hands seem to have a lot of character. . . . These are hands which some day may accomplish great things. . . . These are hands which may some day do marvelous works! They may build mighty bridges, or heal the sick, or hit some homeruns, or write soul-stirring novels! These are hands which may some day change the course of destiny!"

Lucy responds simply, "They've got jelly on them."[5]

Josh Billings had made the same observation: "Man was created a little lower than the angels, and he has been getting a little lower ever since."

The Need for Relationship

So we need to relate to ourselves, to God, and to others. But how? Strangely enough, the answer is by looking beyond ourselves! The only way I receive value from life is by giving myself. The time I come to feel that I have worth is when I show that I care for another person and express this worth in relationship with that person.

Test yourself. In what circumstance have you felt most fulfilled? When do you feel that you have the greatest dignity and value? At what time has life seemed to hold the most meaning for you? The chances are it was at a time of great sacrifice. It may have been that you risked injury to protect another. It could have been when you stayed up all night to minister to the needs of a sick friend. Perhaps it was the time you made a sacrificial gift. In any event, the situation in which you were most fulfilled was, likely, when you were not grasping for yourself but giving for another.

Jesus expresses this truth paradoxically:

"If any man would come after me, let him deny himself and take up his cross and follow me. For whoever would save his life will lose it; and whoever loses his life for my sake and the gospel's will save it" (Mark 8:34–35).

Dr. Karl Menninger, world famous psychiatrist, was presenting a lecture on mental health and answering questions from the audience. "What would you advise a person to do," he was asked, "if that person felt a nervous breakdown coming on?" His reply was rather astonishing: "Lock up your house, go across the railway tracks, find someone in need, and do something to help that person."

A missionary once summarized world thinking as:

Greece said, "Be moderate; know thyself." Rome said, "Be strong, order thyself." Confucianism says, "Be disillusioned; annihilate thyself." Hinduism says, "Be separated; merge thyself." Mohammedanism says, "Be submissive; bend thyself." Modern materialism says, "Be industrious; enjoy thyself." And modern dilettantism says, "Be broad; cultivate thyself." Christianity, on the other hand, says, "Be Christlike, give thyself."

Jesus teaches that the way to find meaningful life and to relate deeply to the center of your own being is to give yourself to God and to others. Even so, we are not properly related to others any more than we are to God. Seeing human need, we commonly pass by on the other side. We are too often those of whom Jesus said:

> " '. . . for I was hungry and you gave me no food, I was thirsty and you gave me no drink, I was a stranger and you did not welcome me, naked and you did not clothe me, sick and in prison and you did not visit me' " (Matthew 25:42, 43).

When did we fail to meet Jesus' needs? He answers, " 'Truly, I say to you, as you did it not to one of the least of these, you did it not to me' " (Matthew 25:45). Jesus obviously teaches that this failure to share is sin. His next words are: "And they will go away into eternal punishment . . ." (Matthew 25:46).

This relationship with others is essential. Jesus even indicates that it should take priority (at least chronologically) over our relationship with God.

> "So if you are offering your gift at the altar, and there remember that your brother has something against you, leave your gift there before the altar and go; first be reconciled to your brother, and then come and offer your gift" (Matthew 5:23-24).

We are instructed even to withhold, temporarily, our worship of almighty God so that we might be related properly with our brothers and sisters. It is only when we are so related with others that we can come to a full and unhindered worship of God.

The Real Meaning of Sin

Matthew reflects Jesus' teaching concerning our failure to relate adequately to God, to ourselves, and to others. This is the real meaning of the word "sin." There can be no sin if there is no God. If I violate the standards established by human law, I am involved in a crime. It is only if there is a God from whose standards I have strayed that I am involved in sinning.

Sin is usurping the place of God. So sin is essentially religious. It is acting or thinking against the will of God. It can be either an evil act or thought or even a good—indeed, a religious—act or thought. Archbishop Temple contended:

There is only one sin, and it is characteristic of the whole world. It is the self-will which prefers 'my' way to God's—which puts 'me' in the centre where only God is in place. It pervades the universe. It accounts for the cruelty of the jungle, where each animal follows its own appetite, unheeding and unable to heed any general good. It becomes conscious, and thereby tenfold more virulent in man—a veritable fall indeed.[6]

What would you say was our Lord's most distinctive teaching about human sin? What was it that he said about sin that was unique—really original? The answer is quite shocking. The sins that he condemned most seriously were *religious* wrongs. Jesus was well received by the common people, the outcasts, those who felt they were not good enough for respectable society. On the other hand, he was disliked and rejected by most of the religious leadership of the day. One significant reason for this reaction was that Jesus was so stern in his criticism of religious pride. Specifically, the three sins that Jesus condemned more than any others were religious demonstration, religious conceit, and religious hypocrisy.

The Sin of Religious Demonstration

The religiously demonstrative were concerned about washing their hands properly before every meal. They were careful to let others know that they gave one-tenth of their income for religious purposes. They prayed ostentatiously at particular hours of the day. They were careful about their diet for religious reasons—and boasted about it. Jesus pointed out that wrong is not so much external as internal. Similarly, he demanded that the heart—not simply external actions—be right.

Jesus made these points in the most dramatic ways. Imagine the feeling of those religious leaders who heard him say:

"Woe to you, scribes and Pharisees, hypocrites! for you cleanse the outside of the cup and of the plate, but inside they are full of extortion and rapacity. . . . you are like whitewashed tombs, which outwardly appear beautiful, but within they are full of dead men's bones and uncleanness. So you also outwardly appear righteous to men, but within you are full of hypocrisy and iniquity" (Matthew 23:25, 27–28).

For Jesus, even religion could be sin.

The Sin of Religious Conceit

Religious conceit was also condemned by Jesus. Humility is the basic attitude to be expressed before God. Jesus told of two men who went up to the temple to pray. One was an exemplary religious man, but he was conceited. Note his prayer: " 'God, I thank thee that I am not like other men, extortioners, unjust, adulterers, or even like this tax collector. I fast twice a week, I give tithes of all that I get' " (Luke 18:11-12). But the other man was socially rejected and felt inadequate before God. Jesus said that this man was "standing far off, would not even lift up his eyes to heaven, but beat his breast, saying, 'God, be merciful to me a sinner!' " (Luke 18:13). And Jesus continued, "I tell you, this man went down to his house justified rather than the other" (Luke 18:14). This conceit, this lack of need for God and presumed goodness, is among the greatest of sins.

The Sin of Religious Hypocrisy

The third sin that Jesus condemned—something of a combination of the other two—is hypocrisy. The hypocrite tries to be viewed as something that he or she is not. The hypocrite is a pretender, a deceiver, an actor.

The sin of hypocrisy is more strongly condemned in the New Testament than any other sin, especially by Jesus. On the other hand, the Greek words *hypocrisy* and *hypocrite* are without ill repute in classical Greek literature. They come from the word meaning "to answer" and relate to a speaker, reader, or actor. In the Bible, however, these words relate to real life, describing the person who acts at living and reflects a "scripted goodness." They describe one who carries evil motives under outer garments of goodness. Note Jesus' words about such people:

> "Thus, when you give alms, sound no trumpet before you, as the hypocrites do in the synagogues and in the streets, that they may be praised by men. . . . And when you pray, you must not be like the hypocrites; for they love to stand and pray in the synagogues and at the street corners, that they may be seen by men. . . . And when you fast, do not look dismal, like the hypocrites, for they disfigure their faces that their fasting may be seen by men. Truly, I say to you, they have their reward" (Matthew 6:2, 5, 16).

Jesus was critical of the hypocrites basically because they had a limited view of God. You cannot fool God who sees beneath the disguise. The One who sees all knows what we really are.

To stop here, however, would be inadequate. We have suggested that Jesus had a high concept of human nature, dignity, and value. On the other hand, we have noted his realistic appraisal of our self-centeredness and sin. This latter emphasis (concerning our sinful nature) is easily misunderstood. Jesus is not interested in a morbid dwelling upon human frailty. His concern is not so much our sin as it is God's love for us while we are still in our sin.

Jesus, God's Shepherd

Thus Jesus tells of a sheep that wandered away but was brought back by the shepherd (Luke 15:3–7); there is the coin that was lost until the woman found it (Luke 15:8–10); and there is the story of the wayward son who went off into a far country and of his father who waited in love (Luke 15:11–32). Jesus indicates that some of us, in our waywardness, move out in ignorance like sheep or wayward sons. Others of us can be lost even when we are not away. We can be like the elder brother in the story of the prodigal son. We can be lost by virtue of circumstances that are not of our own doing as in the story of the lost coin.

The preeminent teaching of Jesus in these stories is that God is ever-loving and ever-seeking us out in love. We should see ourselves, realistically, as sinners and as lost but we should also be like the prodigal who in Jesus' words, "when he came to himself he said . . . 'I will arise and go to my father'" (Luke 15:17–18). When he did, he found that he was loved. He was accepted. He belonged, and life was worthwhile.

This acceptance of the wayward is our acceptance; it speaks to our deepest need. Paul Tillich puts it well:

> Sometimes at that moment a wave of light breaks into our darkness, and it is as though a voice were saying: 'You are accepted. *You are accepted,* accepted by that which is greater than you. . . . Simply accept the fact that you are accepted!'[7]

That is essentially Jesus' teaching concerning what we are. Indeed, that is the essence of all that Jesus was and did—as well as what he taught. In our self–centeredness we are lost; but even in this state we are loved by God. Jesus came to us and for us. When we "accept our acceptance," we find that we are significant. We really belong. We are home; and life is worthwhile.

Chapter Two

What Is God Like?

The Teachings of Jesus Concerning God

—◆—

W hat is God like? What would you say? The answers are many; and many are manifestly false.

The late Dr. J. B. Phillips wrote a little book entitled *Your God is Too Small*.[1] He presents more than a dozen unreal views of God. God is thought by some to be what Phillips calls "a resident policeman," the conscience—the still, small voice—that bothers us when we do something wrong. To others God is a "parental hangover," a remembrance of unhappy thoughts and experiences we had at an early age with our parents. Some spoiled us and granted all our whims. Others nagged and demanded a perfection of which we were not capable. Others see God as a "grand old man." He is a kingly gentleman with a long white beard who sits in heaven—a sort of royal Santa Claus. Phillips' listing includes the "meek and mild," the "absolute perfection," "the heavenly bosom," a "God–in–a–box," a "managing director," and a "second–hand God," among others. To people holding such concepts, Phillips pronounces, "Your God is too small."

The teachings of Jesus concerning God are not so limited. His experience of and teachings about God extend beyond these limited concepts of our day as well as those of the first century. Before turning to what Jesus had to say about God it is profitable to con-

29

sider three historically significant groups who have endeavored to describe God. These include modern thinkers, the pagan thinkers of the ancient world, and the inspired writers of the Hebrew Scriptures. Some of our modern thinkers have endeavored to establish certain arguments that prove, or at least point to, the existence of God. It has been argued, for example, that the universe exists. The thing made points to a Maker. Others have argued that the impressive design reflected in our cosmos shows that there must have been a designer—a heavenly architect—who is God.

These two arguments will not necessarily convince one of a skeptical bent. John Haldane, a scientist, argued with Monsignor Ronald Knox, a Roman Catholic theologian and Bible translator. Haldane argued that it is inevitable that life should appear by chance on at least one of the millions of planets in the universe. Knox remonstrated that Scotland Yard might find a body in the trunk of Haldane's car. Haldane could then argue that out of the millions of automobile trunks in the world, surely one would contain a body. Then Knox concluded, "I think they still would want to know who put it there!"[2]

Greater Than All Argument

Creation is not so much understood with the head as with the whole being. God seeks not our comprehension but our response. James Weldon Johnson, in the rhythm and flow of the black preacher, described creation this way:

> Then God smiled,
> and the light broke,
> and the darkness rolled up on one side,
> and the light stood shining on the other,
> and God said: That's good![3]

It has been suggested that we live in a moral universe that is moving toward good ends; there must then be a moral God who is over it. When we consider these and other arguments, they point toward the existence of God. Nevertheless, they aren't conclusive proof to one who refuses to believe in God. We can't call these arguments scientific proofs in the irrefutable sense. A. J. Cronin wrote about this tension.

At the outset it should be stated that the only motivation power in supernatural faith must be God Himself. God cannot be proved like a mathematical equation, nor can His existence be demonstrated like a problem in a book of Euclid.

Obviously an infinite Being cannot be rationalized in finite terms—our human capacity is utterly incapable of wholly understanding Him. Nevertheless, there are certain simple arguments which help us to discover Him.

If we consider the physical universe, in its mystery and wonder, its order and intricacy, its awe–inspiring immensity, we cannot escape the notion of a primary Creator. Who on a still summer night dares gaze upward at the constellations, glittering in infinity, without the overpowering conviction that such a cosmos came to being through something more than blind indeterminate chance? And our own world, whirling through space in measured rhythm, unfolding its regular progression of the seasons, surely is more than a meaningless ball of matter, thrown off by merest accident from the sun?[4]

God is greater than all proof and argument. We err in assuming that our minds (created by God) are great enough to contain the fullness of God or even prove the existence of God. We find our being in God, not God in us. To be a believer is to know there is a God beyond the top of our heads.

Another significant group to whom we might look are the pagan teachers of the ancient world. The ancient Greeks thought of the gods as being somewhat jealous of human beings and unwilling to help them. These gods were separate from the world and communicated with people only through intermediate demons. The gods were distant and unknown. In some instances, they were even immoral.

The Hebrew Scriptures present a different picture. God was holy and righteous. There was no question about Jahweh's morality. The Lord was presented as a loving God, especially by Hosea. However, this loving was in broad terms—as a sovereign might love the people at large. God could not be approached by an individual with an assurance of acceptance. Moreover, God was independent and could not be limited by human predictions. The God of the Scriptures was far greater and more righteous than the gods of the pagans. But the Almighty was still distant and unknown. Consider, for example, the call of the prophet as recorded in Isaiah 6. The elements reflected in this call are the concerns of the entire book. God is majestic and glorious, demanding repentance and new life. Holy and separate, the holy One is served by intermediate and angelic beings. The modern Christian perception of God's immediacy and involvement with individuals is missing.

Experiencing God

This brings us to the question of what Jesus said about God. It is worthy of noting that Jesus assumed the existence of God. Jesus never argued this matter. Indeed, the entire Bible contains stories about people who have sensed God acting within their experience. They did not feel that it was necessary to prove God's existence. God was there! Jesus lived in fellowship with God and his teaching grew out of this experience.

A. J. Cronin described his initial turning from atheism not as a result of rational argument, but because of the simple witness of God–fearing people in a Welsh mining community.

But I had barely begun my first cup of coffee when I heard a hooter sound the alarm, six long blasts—and almost at once the telephone rang. It was George Conway, secretary of the Medical Aid Society. Briefly he told me that a disaster had occurred in the Ystfad Colliery at Pengelly across the mountain. . . .

When I arrived, 500 men and women had gathered on the outskirts of the pit yard, and there were more outside. They stood in silence, the women mostly in shawls, the men without overcoats. . . . the work was killing. . . . It proceeded in a sort of insane frenzy. . . . "We must go on," Jenkins said with sudden loudness, and a note of hysteria in his voice. "We must go on."

At that moment, when all seemed lost, a faint, unearthly sound was heard in that unfathomable darkness, an almost ghostly tapping. . . .

Slowly, carefully, we brought them out. News of the rescue had preceded us and as we came forth to the surface there arose in a great volume of sound, soberly, yet spontaneously, swelling to the sky from the huge congregation assembled on the troubled wasteland of the Common, that favourite Welsh hymn, "O God, our help in ages past."

It was a moment of emotion that rent the heart, a sight I shall never forget.[5]

We come to faith in God more through witness than by rational argument. Jesus came to reveal, rather than to prove, the Eternal. Thus our relationship with God is more fellowship than absolute comprehension.

Martin Luther King, Jr., learned about God through the preaching of his father and other great ministers in the black tradition. He also involved himself in the studies about God in some of the most sophisticated centers of learning. His doctoral dissertation reflects his insight concerning the nature of God:

> We must conclude that Tillich's "Being Itself" and Weiman's "Creative Event" are lacking in positive religious value. Both concepts are too impersonal to express adequately the Christian conception of God. They provide neither the conditions for true fellowship with God nor the assurance of His goodness.[6]

God as Father

What was new about the teaching of Jesus? What did he say about God that went beyond what was taught by the Old Testament? If we could gather up all of the unique ideas which Jesus presented about God, we might capsulize them all into a very common word—"father." We should recognize that Jesus was not the first person to use the term "father" with reference to God. God was recognized as a father (and as a mother) in the Old Testament. We read, for example, "As a father pities his children, so the Lord pities those who fear him. . . ." (Psalm 103:13); "thou, O Lord art our Father, our Redeemer. . . ." (Isaiah 63:16); "Father of the fatherless and protector of widows is God. . . ." (Psalm 68:5). Jesus was unique not in using "father" with reference to God but in the dimension he poured into the term. Jesus made the image of a father the center of our experience and knowledge of God.

In considering God as Father, we should guard against three rather common errors. First, notice that God is presented as a father, not as a doting grandfather. God is genuinely concerned about us as children. He upholds standards, makes demands, and refuses to spoil us. God reflects a depth of love—not a sloppy sentimentality. The late Oxford don, C. S. Lewis, stated our misdirected desires quite well:

We want, in fact, not so much a Father in Heaven, as a grandfather in Heaven—a senile benevolence who, as they say, 'liked to see young people enjoying themselves,' and whose plan for the universe was simply that it might be truly said at the end of each day, 'a good time was had by all.'[7]

Second, Jesus did not teach that God is Father of all. Creator, yes. Ruler and judge, yes. But Father of all, no—surprising as it may seem. The modern teaching of the "fatherhood of God and brotherhood of man" lacks solid biblical roots. Again, Professor Lewis put it well:

Now the point in Christianity which gives us the greatest shock is the statement that by attaching to Christ we can "become Sons of God." One asks, 'Aren't we Sons of God already? Surely the father-hood of God is one of the main Christian ideas?' Well, in a certain sense, no doubt we are sons of God already. I mean, God brought us into existence and loves us and looks after us, and in that way is like a father. But when the Bible talks of our 'becoming' Sons of God, obviously it must mean something different. And that brings us up against the very center of theology.[8]

Jesus presented the teaching that God is Father only to the twelve disciples. In the earliest Gospel, Mark, God is called "Father" only four times by Jesus. Each of these occasions is found not in his public ministry but in the specific teaching of Jesus to his disciples after they had acknowledged that he was the Christ who had come from God. When he spoke of God as his Father and ours, Jesus reflected genuine personal experience communicated for those who could hear and understand. Jesus did not argue this teaching with his detractors. Nor did he proclaim it broadly to the crowds. It was, rather, shared with those who knew him, who accepted him as having come from God, and who therefore could understand his teaching and relate to his Father.

Third, although Jesus (and biblical writers) teach that God is Father, they do not limit God's nature, characteristics, and actions to those we consider "masculine." Biblically speaking, God is both masculine and feminine and beyond gender limitations.

Christian feminist scholars such as Nancy Hardesty, Virginia Mollenkott, Rosemary Ruether, Letty Russell, Letha Scanzoni, and Phyllis Trible have alerted us to our domination under male-oriented language. The biblical writers lived in social situations that were essentially patriarchal. It is not surprising, therefore, that the authors of the Scriptures referred to God in masculine terms. Indeed, the greater surprise is in noting the extent of the use of feminine language in describing God.

In Isaiah 42:14 God says, 'I will cry out like a woman in travail, I will gasp and pant.' Isaiah 46:3 continues the image: 'Hearken to me, O House of Jacob, all the remnant of the House of Israel, who have been borne by me from your birth, carried from the womb.' Again in Isaiah 49:15, God asks Israel, 'Can a woman forget her sucking child, that she should have no compassion on the son of her womb? Even these may forget, yet I will not forget you.' The same image is used in Isaiah 66:13 where God promises, 'As one whom his mother comforts, so I will comfort you' (all of which might lead one to ask if "Second Isaiah" was really Isaiah's wife, the prophetess). The psalmist also sees God as a mother when he says, 'I have calmed and quieted my soul, like a child quieted at its mother's breast' (Psalm 131:2).[9]

Unfortunately, Bible translators have been children of their own times and have inaccurately translated portions of the Bible using masculine language not included in the original Hebrew, Aramaic, or Greek texts. Such inaccurate translations are currently in the process of modification. A new edition of the Revised Standard Version of the Bible will appear in 1990. The translations committee of this new edition has committed itself to drop masculine language that is not reflected in the original. Nevertheless, Professor Bruce Metzger, chair of the committee, has stated, "We are not going to change references to God where the masculine pronoun is in the text. We fool ourselves if we launder the language." The committee is concerned, and rightly, with ridding the Revised Standard Version of inappropriately male–biased language by accurately translating the Bible, not by rewriting it.

So what *is* involved in this teaching of Jesus that God is Father? It is obvious that Jesus was not arguing a point. Nor was he creating a system of thought to explain the universe. Rather, he spoke out of that clear understanding of God that was deep within his own experience. He was communicating relationship. He shared this experience and understanding in order that others would sense God in the intimacy of relationship expressed in the term "father."

It is important to recognize here that religious teaching and theology grow out of vital religious experience. Christian doctrine does not create vital Christian experience; doctrine rather reflects systematically and rationally such experience. Thus Frederick Buechner says,

> It is not objective proof of God's existence that we want but, whether we use religious language for it or not, the experience of God's presence. That is the miracle that we really get.[10]

No Limit to Love

What then are the implications of this teaching? First, Jesus' presentation of God as Father means that God loves us all. This is basic to Jesus' teaching and to the Christian faith. Missionary E. Stanley Jones once asked Mahatma Gandhi how the Christian faith might become more indigenous to India and thus contribute to the improvement of that nation. Gandhi responded:

> I would suggest, first, that all of the Christians must begin to live more like Jesus Christ. Second, I would suggest that you must practice your religion without adulterating or toning it down. Third, I would suggest that you must put your emphasis on love, for love is the centre and soul of Christianity.[11]

This understanding of the universal love of God may seem commonplace to us, but it was a shocking thing in the ancient world. The Jewish people sensed that they were the people of God and found it difficult to believe that God could love an unworthy, heathen world. Nor were they the only exclusively-minded people in ancient society. The Greeks referred to all other people as "barbarians." Today the Moslem world refers to all people who are not of the creed of Islam as "infidels." Christians have not been blameless in the disparagement of others either. We speak of the "outsiders" in one term or another. But Jesus saw God as Father who loves and is gracious to all, regardless of national, racial, social, or economic backgrounds. There is no limit to the love of God. This love involves us. If God loves all people, God certainly loves you and me.

Second, if God loves all of us, God loves each of us. The love of God is universal, but it is also personal. In the Hebrew Bible God is seen as the father of Israel. God was the father of individuals only as they happened to be members of the larger family of the nation. But in the teaching of Jesus God loves each child. Jesus reflected this concern of God for individuals with his statement that "even the hairs of your head are all numbered" (Matthew 10:30; Luke 12:7). Is not God like the concerned shepherd? What shepherd "having a hundred sheep, if he has lost one of them, does not leave the ninety-nine in the wilderness, and go after the one which is lost, until he finds it?" (Luke 15:4). So, Jesus said, "there is joy before the angels of God over one sinner who repents" (Luke 15:10). It is at this point, perhaps more than any other, where Jesus reveals in his actions what God is like. Jesus constantly sought out and helped needy persons.

Third, the understanding of God as Father shows that God is at once concerned and close enough to be involved with our needs. This concept came as a surprise to those in the ancient world. The Greeks saw God as being far above the world, too concerned with ultimate perfection to be involved in blood, sweat, misery, and death. The people of the Old Testament saw God as exalted high above all, the Eternal who contacted humanity only through angels and other intermediaries. But when Jesus taught that God is Father, he meant that God cared. God is more concerned than are human parents. Remember Jesus' words, "If you then, who are evil, know how to give good gifts to your children, how much more will the heavenly Father give the Holy Spirit to those who ask him!" (Luke 11:13).

If we could accept this sense of God's concern and interest in our welfare, we could find ourselves much healthier. Much of our frustration—our stewing about problems that never develop, our fretting and worrying about those things we cannot change, our helpless grasping for that which we cannot achieve—could be diminished greatly by an effective belief that God is concerned. (Jesus also taught that God is close, because he experienced God as close, as should we.) This concern of God is expressed in action, in seeking us out. Recall our Lord's stories in Luke 15 which picture God as an anxious father, a faithful shepherd, and a searching woman.

C. G. Mountefiore, a renowned Jewish scholar, suggested early in this century that "this direct search for and appeal to the sinner are new and moving notes of high import and significance." He further said that Jesus sought out sinners which "was a new and sublime contribution to the development of religion." Indeed, no one had so clearly seen God as concerned, loving, seeking, until Jesus taught and lived this type of concern.

It is significant to note that the teachings of Jesus concerning God's active, seeking love grew out of his own being and experience. These teachings are the creation, not the creator, of the love that Jesus experienced from God.

> For love is not genuinely expressed in self–sacrificial actions whose purpose is simply to express love. It is revealed in costly actions undertaken to accomplish something vitally important which love sees to be necessary. A man would not be revealing his love for his wife if he made a bonfire in the garden and burnt himself on it, explaining that he was doing this for her sake! But if the house was on fire, and while rescuing his wife he incurred first degree burns from which he later died in dreadful agony—losing his life, not because he was trying to, but because the situation was so desperate that it came to this—then his self-sacrifice would indeed reveal the measure of his love for her. And Christ's death was undergone *for* mankind, not just as a meaningless gesture but as something that became practically probable and then inevitable as he steadfastly adhered to his vocation.[12]

Finally, the teaching of Jesus that God is a father means that we can be open and honest in our religious experience and expression. We don't stand on formality within a family. Those elements of ceremony and ritualism which may be necessary to impress others are not necessary to impress our Father—if we really understand God to be one who loves. The relationship can be just this open. This intimacy includes the working through of problems, needs, and hidden desires together. We are free to approach the Almighty. We can deal with areas of our experience of which we are so ashamed that we are normally dishonest about them. The word of Jesus should lead us to be open enough to admit when we are wrong but trusting enough to know that the one who is all–knowing is also all–loving.

Jesus even called God "Abba, Father" (Mark 14:36). The word, *abba*, is Aramaic, the language Jesus spoke to his disciples. Why did Paul write this word to the Roman Christians (Romans 8:15) who, in all likelihood, had never heard this language before? He may have used it because the Christians throughout the Roman world had learned the meaning of this Aramaic word and used it in their own language of prayer. The concept of God as Father was expressed naturally in this word. The idea cannot be translated adequately; it is something like "daddy" or "papa." Only a child in dependent spirit would use the term. No one else would think of employing such an expression.

What does this teaching of Jesus mean to us in our day? Do you find yourself reading these words with desire but disbelief? Do you find it hard to believe that the eternal, infinite God who has made and who holds together all the vastness of space is interested in you personally? You would do well to consider the authority of the one person who really knew. He spoke out of a deep experience of relationship with God. He says that we can know God in this relationship, too. Do you find it hard to believe? A more important question is, Do you find that you really want to believe? It can be. God is love. The eternal Father loves all people. In particular, God loves you.

> I know not where His islands lift
> Their fronded palms in air;
> I only know I cannot drift
> Beyond His love and care.[13]
> —John Greenleaf Whittier

Chapter Three

Love: What Is It, Really?

The Teachings of Jesus Concerning Love

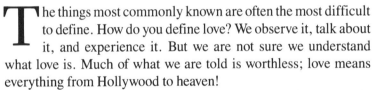

The things most commonly known are often the most difficult to define. How do you define love? We observe it, talk about it, and experience it. But we are not sure we understand what love is. Much of what we are told is worthless; love means everything from Hollywood to heaven!

The adolescent experience of "puppy love" is exciting but rarely deep. Henry Ward Beecher described it aptly: "Young love is a flame—very pretty—often very hot and fierce, but still only light and flickering."

It is far more touching to observe a couple who have loved and grown together across the years. As Beecher said further, "The love of the older and disciplined heart is as coals, deep burning, unquenchable."

The day after Jack Benny died in December, 1974, a long-stemmed red rose was delivered to his wife of 48 years, Mary Livingston Benny. Each day thereafter, a single rose arrived. After several weeks Mary inquired as to who sent them.

David Jones, the florist, explains:

"I told Mary that quite a while before Jack passed away, he stopped into my shop to send a bouquet of flowers to a friend. As he was leaving, he suddenly turned back and said: 'David, if anything happens to me, I want you to send my doll a red rose every day.'

"When I related Jack's conversation, there was complete silence. I could tell she was crying as she thanked me and said goodbye." Subsequently, Mary learned that Jack actually had included a provision for her flowers in his will. One red rose was to be delivered to her . . . *for the rest of her life.* [1]

Love is necessary to human development. Love is needed, for example, in the family. Our basic social unit is breaking down rapidly. The main reason?—Lack of love! Love is needed by all, especially by children. As many run afoul of our social, moral, or legal standards, it is becoming increasingly apparent that the primary reason is a lack of love and support in the home. When one is not emotionally balanced, psychologists often relate the imbalance to a lack of love in childhood. To be human is to need love.

Maturity of relationships is needed among human beings from the individual to the international level. If not love, then at least elemental justice is necessary in interpersonal relationships. Such justice can develop into trust which, in turn, may even beget love. In any event, the future of humanity is threatened by our refusal to engage seriously in rational international dialogue. Never before have we so desperately needed a relationship of mutual understanding among nations.

The Model of God's Love

Although it is largely not recognized, our need for love has been met. Love has been communicated clearly and demonstrated effectively to a needy humanity. The message has come from one who exemplified it better than any who ever walked this earth. Indeed, he showed love far more than he explained it. "Greater love has no man than this, that a man lay down his life for his friends" (John 15:13). It is surprising that Jesus said so little about love. He communicated more about love through demonstrations than words. His statements were few and brief but meaningful.

First, he told us to love God with all that we are. This was the essence of the *Shema,* the daily prayer of every Jewish man (Deuteronomy 6:4, 5). Second, Jesus added the teaching of Leviticus that we should love our neighbors as ourselves (Leviticus

19:18). These two teachings are not combined in the Old Testament, but Jesus recognized them as a summary of the demands of the Scriptures. Together they constituted "the whole law."

Living by these teachings was and is not easy. Even the first disciples found it difficult to do so. Mark tells us that Jesus once asked his disciples, " 'What were you discussing on the way?' But they were silent; for on the way they had discussed with one another who was the greatest" (Mark 9:33-34). Some love this—each wanting to be the greatest! Two of them wanted to sit on Jesus' right hand and on his left, respectively. The remaining disciples were angry. They resented those who wanted the chief positions. Their anger, however, revealed their own jealousy and self-seeking.

Recall how Jesus washed the feet of his disciples in the upper room. Why did he do it? The obvious answer is that none of them was willing to wash the feet of another. So—if we find it hard to love, we should recognize that the early disciples found it equally difficult.

There are problems involved in loving the way we should. It is not the normal thing to do. The normal thing is to demand our rights. The "sensible" person will tell you to be independent. It is hard truly to love because love is sharing. It is relinquishing "rights" and sacrificing independence.

Moreover, true loving is a gamble. It wouldn't be a gamble, of course, if we were all loving. The fact is that people are self-centered and unloving, especially at the international level. Shall we simply say, "Well, let's treat the Russians with love; let's be nice to Castro; let's empty our penitentiaries out of love. Then all of these people will respond in kind." Yes—but *what* kind? Radical love is a gamble. It may not work. It may not get us what we want. What did love get Jesus but a cross! Let's be honest about it. Love costs; it hurts, and is a gamble.

Isn't this why we think of love as being limited to that which is for our own good? Isn't this why we popularize romantic love? Don't we love those to whom we are attracted?

The Great Commandment

What did Jesus teach about love that is so different from this concept? What was it that he meant by love? He was approached by a religious leader who asked:

> ". . . which is the great commandment in the law?" And he said to him, "You shall love the Lord your God with all your heart, and with all your soul, and with all your mind. This is the great and first commandment. And a second is like it, You shall love your neighbor as yourself. On these two commandments depend all the law and the prophets" (Matthew 22:36–40).

So Jesus taught that we should love completely at two levels— first, God; and second, our neighbor. Both of these teachings are taken from the Hebrew Scriptures. In the Old Testament, these two statements are in different books, but Jesus brought them together as the one great commandment. Indeed, he said that these two commands to love are the crux of the entire Hebrew Bible. "On these two commandments," he said, "depend *all* the law and the prophets" (author's emphasis).

The melancholy Danish Christian philosopher, Soren Kierkegaard, asked and answered the question: "What does it mean to love one's neighbor?

> To love one's neighbor means, while remaining within the earthly distinctions allotted to one, essentially to will to exist equally for every human being without exception. . . .
> But when the curtain falls, the one who played the king, and the one who played the beggar, and all the others—they are quite alike, all one and the same: actors. . . . And when in death the curtain falls on the stage of actuality . . . then they also are all one; they are human beings."[2]

To love my neighbor is to recognize that my neighbor is a human being created by God. I should not force my neighbor to earn my love. I should be pleased if the other person is kind, courteous, educated, and sensitive. I should similarly be pleased if the full potential of my neighbor is realized in a fruitful occupation. Nevertheless, the basis of neighbor love is the identification in a common humanity, not in individual achievements.

It isn't easy to love your neighbor. What is the secret? C. S. Lewis has come as close as any to the answer:

The rule for all of us is perfectly simple. Do not waste time bothering whether you 'love' your neighbor; act as if you did. As soon as we do this, we find one of the great secrets. When you are behaving as if you loved someone, you will presently come to love him.[3]

Such action on behalf of my neighbor is contingent upon my recognizing our relationship as neighbors. I cannot and will not act in a loving way toward a person whom I ignore, refuse to recognize, or avoid. Charles Lamb once said, "Don't introduce me to that man! I want to go on hating him, and I can't hate a man whom I know."

These are only first steps. Jesus calls you not only to love your neighbor but to "love your neighbor *as yourself*" (author's emphasis). This step involves a movement toward my neighbor with concern. "Tell me how much you know of the sufferings of your fellow men and I will tell you how much you have loved them," said Helmut Thielicke.[4]

Am I therefore to overlook the flaws in a person's character? Is such love blind to faults? Hardly. Christian teachers have been saying for years that we must hate a person's evil actions but we must not hate the person. We are told that we, like God, are to hate the sin but not the sinner. C. S. Lewis affirms this teaching, but with a helpful clarification:

For a long time I used to think this is a silly, straw-splitting distinction: how could you hate what a man did and not hate the man? But years later it occurred to me that there was one man to whom I had been doing this all my life—namely myself. However much I might dislike my own cowardice or conceit or greed, I went on loving myself. There had never been the slightest difficulty about it. In fact the very reason why I hated the things was that I loved the man. Just because I loved myself, I was sorry to find that I was the sort of man who did those things.[5]

Appropriate self-love is as difficult as neighbor love. An inappropriate self-love is self-aggrandizement, and the essence of sin. Appropriate love of self, on the other hand, is genuine self-acceptance and the essence of the gospel. God has accepted us freely and fully in Jesus Christ. This limitless love affair of God is the basis of appropriate self-love.

Carl Gustav Jung contended that:

the acceptance of one's self is the essence of the moral problem and the acid test of one's whole outlook on life. That I feed the beggar, that I forgive an insult, that I love my enemy in the name of Christ— all these are undoubtedly great virtues. What I do unto the least of my brethren, that I do unto Christ. But what if I should discover that the least amongst them all, the poorest of all beggars, the most impudent of all offenders, yea the very fiend himself—that these are within me, and that I myself stand in need of the alms of my own kindness, that I myself am the enemy who must be loved—what then? Then, as a rule, the whole thrust of Christianity is reversed: there is then no more talk of love and long-suffering; we say to the brother within us, "Raca," and condemn and rage against ourselves. We hide him from the world, we deny ever having met this least among the lowly in ourselves, and had it been God himself who drew near to us in this despicable form we should have denied him a thousand times before a single cock had crowed.[6]

The love of God and neighbor becomes a summary of God's demand, because the command to love God and our neighbor with all that we are is going beyond any rules that we can establish. There were commandments against murder, stealing, adultery, lying, and similar wrongs. The fact is, however, that if we love our neighbor completely we will not kill. Moreover, we will not steal, nor will we lie or commit other wrongs against our neighbor. And certainly, if we love God with utter personal devotion we shall sense the divine presence at all times. Then our desire will be fellowship with God rather than the artificial freedom of breaking some moral law.

"Love Your Enemies"

These teachings, important as they are, are still expanded by Jesus. He added a third demand concerning our love. We should even love our enemies. Here is the radical teaching of Jesus. After all, he said, we all love our friends and those who treat us right. So where are we different from anyone else if we only love those who love us and who act as our friends? Love of our enemies is at the heart of the gospel. Jesus' teaching at this point becomes uniquely Christian. If you are to be like Jesus Christ—if you are to understand what God is like, giving the only begotten for sinners—then you must learn to love your enemies. This love of God for those who have rejected the cosmic Lover is unique. It is a different kind of love. It goes out to all the world. It is a love that is undeserved. It is a self-giving of the One who loves, rather than the deserving of the one who is loved. Even if the person who is loved does not appreciate this love, it still continues.

This undemanding love was explicated by the Swedish theologian, Anders Nygren, who differentiated between *Eros* as a grasping, self-seeking love and *Agape* as an out-going, self-giving love.[7] It is no secret that the teachings of the New Testament and of Nygren concerning love go far beyond the popular understandings of our day. Donald Capps, of Princeton, observed this point with tongue-in-cheek:

> There was a young pastor in Flanders
> Whose expert on love was Ann Landers
> He refused a free copy
> of Nygren's *Eros and Agape*
> "Hier stehe ich,
> ich kann nicht Anders."[8]
> *Here I stand; I cannot (do) other.*

Current popular mood to the contrary, true love is self-giving, even sacrificial. If you love a beautiful woman or a handsome man; if you love a person who is always kind and loving to you; if you love a person who meets your needs and grants your desires and enriches your personality; what's so special about that? Such love just comes naturally. But if you love someone who is unacceptable and doesn't care; if you love someone who constantly rejects you and makes you miserable; if you love someone who lets you know that you are unloved; if you love that person with the ugly disposition and negative personality; then you are different! You really love—not because the person is lovable but because you are loving. Now if you experienced God's love in Jesus Christ while you were still estranged from God, you may show this love to others and, even, love your enemies.

Helmut Thielicke illustrated the point by telling this story.

In one of the newer apartment houses which are so flimsy that everything can be heard, there is a row going on because one of the tenants always has his radio on at top volume. In the apartment house there lived an old, wise, very philanthropically minded man who talked to one of the more exasperated tenants in the attempt to calm him down. After a long discussion he told him as a last resort how to get along with radio–neighbors in such a situation: 'Yes, you really have to love people in order to put up with them.' 'You mean to say,' said the other, 'that I should love a fellow who turns on jazz music at full volume every night at twelve o'clock?' Whereupon the old man replied, 'Well, it's no trick at all to love someone who has no radio.'[9]

One of the earliest Christian documents to be written after the New Testament was the *Didache,* "The Teaching of the Twelve Apostles." The *Didache* describes the Christian response to "those who curse you," "your enemies," and "those who persecute you." It asks, "what credit is it to you if you love those who love you? Is that not the way the heathen act?" Rather, "you must love those who hate you," and as a result, "you will make no enemies." Some have translated this last clause as, "you will *have* no enemies."[10]

This latter translation is reflected in the response of Abe Lincoln to the question of an elderly woman when he was asked, "How can you speak kindly of your enemies when you should rather destroy them?" "Madam," he said, "do I not destroy them when I make them my friends?"

The teaching of our Lord concerning love of enemies appears at first to be unrealistic. But it reflects more realism than it may appear to at first. C. S. Lewis indicates that:

> My self–love makes me think myself nice, but thinking myself nice is not why I love myself. So loving my enemies does not apparently mean thinking them nice either. That is an enormous relief.[11]

Professor Thielicke of the University of Hamburg calls to our attention a scene in Erich Maria Remarque's book about World War I, *All Quiet on the Western Front:*

> The author describes an assault in which at one point, when they had come in contact with the enemy, he leaped into a shell hole. In the shell hole he found an Englishman. After the first shock of fright he considered what he should do now. Should they proceed to bayonet

each other? But this bit of reflection was soon ended when he saw the other man was severely wounded, so badly wounded that the German soldier was humanly touched by his condition. He gave him a drink from his canteen and the man gave him a look of gratitude. The Englishman then indicated that he wanted him to open his breast pocket. He did so and an envelope containing pictures of the man's family fell out. He obviously wanted to look at them once more. In that moment before the English soldier died, the German held up before him the pictures of his wife, his children, and his mother.[12]

This loving of our enemies is closely related to Jesus' demand for forgiveness. We must forgive those who have wronged us. We must take the initiative in seeking out the person with whom we have had a disagreement. Jesus strongly urged us to be reconciled with others in every relationship. He even went so far as to say, "For if you forgive men their trespasses, your heavenly Father also will forgive you; but if you do not forgive men their trespasses, neither will your Father forgive your trespasses" (Matthew 6:14, 15). Why won't God forgive me when I am unforgiving? Doesn't God love me anyhow? Yes—but not me only. God loves every person, including my so-called enemy. So I must love even my enemy if I am to be like God who is love.

This teaching centers upon the essence of love. It is deeply personal, relational, and even emotional. The essence of love is not essentially cognitive or theoretical. Horace Mann, an eminent nineteenth-century American educator, risked his political future by advocating support of common schools. Mann once delivered an address at the opening of a reformatory for boys. He made the statement that if only one boy were saved from ruin it would pay for all the costs, care, and labor of establishing such an institution. Later, in private, a man tested Mann: "Did you not color that a little when you said all the expense and labor would be repaid if it saved one boy?" "Not if it was my boy," replied Mann.[13]

Dr. Gene Bartlett is admired widely as a great American Baptist preacher and past president of the American Baptist Churches in the U.S.A. He describes the effectiveness of personal concern:

Empathy in its way is therapy. It strangely helps alleviate suffering. After these many years I can recall a way my father had of comforting one of us when some hurt had come. When we ran to him with some minor injury, a bump or a cut, often weeping with pain, he rarely said, "Oh, come on now! That isn't much!" He never admonished, as I recall, "Big boys don't cry!" But it was not uncommon for him to stop his work, listen to the story, perhaps look at the injury and simply say, "That *really* hurts!" A strange response when you think of it. It told us nothing we did not really know. After all, it was our hurt, not his. Yet one always felt helped! It was a *response*. You knew you had been heard. Someone else was sharing the hurt with you, and that knowledge helped.[14]

This love is reflected more simply and pointedly in the story of the girl who came home from a neighbor's house where her young friend had died. "Why did you go?" asked her father. "To comfort her mother," the child responded. "What could you do to comfort her?" "I climbed into her lap and cried with her."

The New Commandment

Now we should note a fourth and final command of Jesus concerning love. We have seen how he combined two ancient teachings—love of God and love of neighbor—into what he called "the great commandment." We have also noted his new and radical teaching of love for enemies as it is rooted in the good news of God's love for us. Now we approach Jesus' fourth teaching about love, which he calls the "new commandment." It is found in the fourth Gospel and is not clearly spelled out in the first three. This new commandment is that we should love all Christians as our sisters and brothers.

The love of siblings is not always apparent and is often the butt of jokes. Sam Levenson was fond of saying, "They sure get along like brothers—Cain and Abel." James Dent made this same point in the *Charleston Gazette* with a story about a minister who was speaking to a Sunday church school class about the things money can't buy. "It can't buy laughter and it can't buy love," he told them. Driving his point home, he said, "What would you do if I offered you a thousand dollars not to love your mother and father?" Stumped silence ensued. Finally, a small voice queried, "How much would you give me not to love my big sister?"

Jesus assumed that everyone who followed him was a sister or brother to every other follower of the Way. Moreover, he demanded that we relate as siblings should. "A new commandment I give to you, that you love one another; even as I have loved you, that you also love one another. By this all men will know that you are my disciples, if you have love for one another" (John 13:34, 35). Here is the great mark of a Christian. Non–Christians will recognize our devotion to Christ—not primarily by our knowledge, our ability, our zeal, our piety, or our purity—but if we "love one another."

Once I see Jesus' fourfold demand that I love God, my neighbor, my enemy, and my Christian brother or sister, an obvious question still remains. How do I go about it? How do I get this love? Consider this: It is Jesus who makes the demands and it is he from whom we should learn how to love. The first thing that Jesus teaches us in this regard is to recognize the potential value in any person. He always did.

There was a woman who was obviously a sinner and who was rejected by her entire community. Because she felt accepted by Jesus we read that, "weeping, she began to wet his feet with her tears, and wiped them with the hair of her head, and kissed his feet, and anointed them with the ointment" (Luke 7:38). The people around—including Jesus' host of the moment—were critical of the woman but Jesus treated her with respect and, even, honor.

There was a tax collector named Zacchaeus. He was hated by the public. But Jesus recognized his potential, and he said, "he also is a son of Abraham" (Luke 19:9). If we are to learn to love, then we must begin by seeing the potential dignity of all people—including that of socially unacceptable persons.

Second, if we claim to be followers of Jesus Christ, we must see the value of every person in God's eyes. This concept includes an acceptance of ourselves and an appreciation of the value God puts upon us. While we must always recognize our sin and self–centeredness, it is crucial that we know our acceptance in Christ.

Within this acceptance born of grace, we must accept and affirm others. Moreover, we must communicate this at a personal level. I've heard Andrew Young describe the hug of his grandmother who repeatedly said, "You ain't no nigger baby. You're God's chile!"

Can you honestly reject any person for whom Jesus Christ died?

Can you feel that anyone is unworthy when God looks upon that person as God's own child? If so—and this is both serious and biblical—how can you justify the claim that Jesus Christ is your Lord?

Third, and mark it well, in order to love, you must be committed to Jesus Christ. We can learn to love people as we share the love of Jesus Christ within our own experience. Peter learned to forgive, because the forgiveness of Christ engulfed his life. He became a great leader as the power of Christ developed within him. So we may become loving as the love of Jesus Christ for others becomes the primary thrust within our experience. How can you learn to love as Christ does?—From him as he lives anew within your experience.

Now, back to our initial question: "How do you define love?" The gospel is concerned with describing love rather than defining it. We have been loved. Christ has died for us. Now we respond in love. The secret, we find, is that love is a giving, not a getting. It is loving both God who is worthy and all who may not be worthy.

Jesus' teaching about love gathers up what had been taught before and brings the new dimension of his own person into the picture. This summary helps us to see how he is both the fulfillment of what is found in the Old Testament and of the good news of God's breaking into our experience. Jesus tells us that we are to love God with everything we have. So did the Hebrew Scriptures. Jesus tells us that we must love our neighbors as ourselves. So does the Old Testament. But Jesus also adds that we come into a new relationship with God and with every other Christian. We must love each of these sisters and brothers in Christ and thereby show our oneness with them and with God. This is a new relationship. This is the gospel as it speaks to our relationship with every Christian throughout the world.

Finally, and most dramatically, Jesus commands us to love our enemies. This loving can be done if we recognize that God loved us when we were enemies. Jesus Christ came to die for me when I was in desperate need—estranged from God, lost, and without hope.

If you can accept the fact that God has loved you when you were unworthy of that love, you may become one who really loves your enemies. Harry Emerson Fosdick called our attention to a dramatic expression of this kind of love:

> In the course of the Armenian atrocities a young woman and her brother were pursued down the street by a Turkish soldier, cornered in an angle of the wall, and the brother was slain before his sister's eyes. She dodged down an alley, leaped over a wall, and escaped. Later, being a nurse, she was forced by the Turkish authorities to work in the military hospital. Into her ward was brought, one day, the same Turkish soldier who had slain her brother. He was very ill. A slight inattention would insure his death. The young woman, now safe in America, confesses to the bitter struggle that took place in her mind. The old Adam cried "Vengeance"; and the new Christ cried "Love." And, equally to the man's good and to her own, the better side of her conquered, and she nursed him as carefully as any other patient in the ward. The recognition had been mutual and one day, unable longer to restrain his curiosity, the Turk asked his nurse why she had not let him die, and when she replied, "I am a follower of him who said, 'Love your enemies and do them good,' " he was silent for a long time. At last he spoke: "I never knew that there was such a religion. If that is your religion tell me more about it, for I want it."[15]

There it is. That is the way Jesus Christ lived. This is the gospel: God loves you just the way you are—even in your sin. God wants you to accept the fact that you are loved and that Jesus Christ has died for you. And then God wants you to love every other person for the sake of Jesus Christ. God wants you to love every Christian everywhere as your brother or sister. And God wants you to love others in the earnest hope that they, too, will become God's children.

Chapter Four

Money: Is
It Good or Evil?

The Teachings of Jesus Concerning Money

D o we need to argue that money alone does not bring happiness? Hardly! So many who have seemingly unlimited wealth are still unhappy. Many of those who take their own lives in our day come from this class. There are those Marilyn Monroes with wealth, recognition, and glamour who find life to be without meaning. On the other hand, there are the John Kennedys who also seem to have everything, but find real meaning in life through service to humanity. And there are the many who find significance in sacrifice—not in comfort. A classic example in our century is Mother Teresa of Calcutta who has given her life and ministry to the "poorest of the poor." On occasion, entire nations are called to sacrifice, and we unite in self-giving. Remember Churchill's words? "I have never promised anything but blood, toil, sweat, and tears."

Sacrifice does not come easily, however. We enjoy telling stories about those who are overly thrifty, probably because we are ourselves so concerned about money. The late Jack Benny made a fortune telling stories about his own alleged miserly qualities. George Burns recalls an occasion when he "one-upped" the master miser.

There was the time he and I were having lunch at the Brown Derby, and he couldn't decide whether or not to put butter on his bread. He said, "You know, I hate bread without butter." "Well, put butter on it then," I said. "I can't," he sighed. "Mary put me on a diet and she said no butter." "Then eat it without butter." "But I *love* butter. Bread is nothing without butter." "So put butter on it." "I better call Mary." "Jack, please, make this one decision yourself!" Well, he had butter, and when the check came for the lunch, I said, "Give it to Jack Benny." "Why should I pay the check?" Jack asked. "Because," I said, "if you don't, I'll tell Mary you had butter."[1]

Jokes about miserly people are not limited to Americans. Bulgarians, for example, like to tell "tightwad" jokes about the citizens of the Bulgarian city of Gabrovo. They claim that Gabrovians are so miserly that they stop their clocks at night to keep the gears from wearing out. When they talk in the evenings, they turn out the lights since they can hear just as well in the dark. They purchase doughnuts with large holes since the holes are free. When they buy a fish, they demand that it be wrapped in today's paper. A young Gabrovian boasted that he saved money by running behind the bus instead of riding. His father responded, "You could have saved more money by running behind a taxi!"

We can chuckle at such stories, inasmuch as we know that money isn't everything. Even so, we often act as if it is. "Money isn't everything," we say, "but it's way ahead of whatever is in second place."

Chicago's Judge Kelly is reputed to have said, "My friends, money is not all. It is not money that will mend a broken heart or reassemble the fragments of a dream. Money cannot brighten the hearth nor repair the portals of a shattered home. I refer, of course, to Confederate money!" We accept such statements as humorous because they are no more than exaggerations of the way we act. We admire and envy persons because they drive Cadillacs, Lincolns, or Rolls Royces.

It is no secret that financial remuneration and the worth of a person's work are not properly related in our society. During a speech in Pittsburgh, West Virginia's Senator Robert Byrd defended legislation that raised a congressional representative's pay from $44,600 to $57,500. To dramatize his point he whipped off his dinner jacket, uncased his fiddle, and presented a hoedown render-

ing of "Rye Whiskey" and "Cumberland Gap." Once his profes-
sional audience overcame their initial surprise, they joined in
applause and foot–stomping. Then Byrd said, "Remember, you'd
think nothing of paying a hillbilly musician that $57,500!"

It is not surprising that some thoughtful people in our day have
"copped out," forsaking the system. They see the vanity of mis-
placed values. Nor is it surprising that other nations do not love our
country. They see the hollowness of the materialistic American
outlook. Money, gadgets, technological advances, *things*—these
are rapidly replacing the basic human values on which our great
nation was founded.

Some years ago we reflected our vanity with a popular song
which stated, "Money Is the Root of All the Evil." This is, of
course, a misquotation of the Bible. The Bible does not claim
money to be the root of all evil. On the contrary, it is the *love* of
money that is the root of all evils (1 Timothy 6:10). Even this is not
a quotation of Jesus. So what did Jesus say about money?

The Eye of a Needle

If we are to understand clearly the teachings of Jesus with reference to material wealth, we might well begin with what he did *not*
teach. He did not teach much that we might expect; nor did he
teach much of what we have assumed.

First, contrary to the assumptions of some, Jesus did not teach
any particular economic theory. He did not come to us as a sociolo-
gist, a philosopher, or an economist. He espounded neither social-
istic nor capitalistic theory. He did not identify with the Sadducees
or Herodians who profited from their great land holdings; nor did
he belong to the Essenes who lived in communes under central
control. Jesus came, rather, to tell us how we might know God and
how we might live in fellowship with our Maker. Indeed, this is the
purpose of the entire Bible.

We must take care to note that this purpose does not eliminate the
relevance of Jesus' teachings to social, economic, and political
areas. When Jesus spoke of our knowledge of God and of our living
in relationship with God, he dealt with the whole of our lives—
including the economic areas. There is no particularly religious or

theological portion of our personalities. We are whole people living in a real world. If we have a vital relationship with God, this relationship is reflected in all areas of our lives.

Jesus came speaking to and giving himself for our freedom. We are to become free personally, religiously, socially, and economically. He wants us to be free from the oppression of extreme poverty. Moreover, he wants us to be free from that greedy, grasping spirit to which we are too prone in our materialistic age.

Inasmuch as Jesus did not speak as an economic theorist, we cannot establish the superiority of any one economic system on the basis of his teachings. Economic systems grow out of social situations—not out of the Bible.

Second, Jesus did not teach that wealth is the direct result of spiritual superiority or of the blessing of God. Jesus went so far as to say that "it is easier for a camel to go through the eye of a needle than for a rich man to enter the kingdom of God" (Matthew 19:24).

On another occasion Jesus pointed out how far a rich man might be from a knowledge of God. "Take heed," he said, "and beware of all covetousness; for a man's life does not consist in the abundance of his possessions" (Luke 12:15). He illustrated this point, as he often did, by telling a story:

> "The land of a rich man brought forth plentifully; and he thought to himself, 'What shall I do, for I have nowhere to store my crops?' And he said, 'I will do this: I will pull down my barns, and build larger ones; and there I will store all my grain and my goods. And I will say to my soul, Soul, you have ample goods laid up for many years; take your ease, eat, drink, be merry.' But God said to him, 'Fool! This night your soul is required of you; and the things you have prepared, whose will they be?' So is he who lays up treasure for himself, and is not rich toward God" (Luke 12:16–21).

It is obvious that one can be rich in goods but "not rich in the eyes of God" (Phillips). Relationship with God is what counts. To accept less is to play the fool.

Third—and this seems the opposite of what was just stated—Jesus did not consider money, wealth, and material things to be wrong. It is both appropriate and just to receive fair payment for services rendered. After Clarence Darrow had delivered a client from legal troubles, the client exclaimed rhetorically, "How can I ever show my appreciation?" Darrow replied, "Ever since the Phoenicians invented money there has only been one answer to that question!" Material rewards were not reflected as evil either in Jesus' actions or teachings.

The Dead Sea Scrolls were discovered several decades ago. These scrolls reflect a community of Jewish people who withdrew from the society of their time. They thought of the power structures of their own day—financial, social, and religious—as evil. These people went out in the desert and created their own community. Jesus was not part of this community. Indeed, he was not even like John the Baptist who lived in the desert and rejected so much of the society of the first century. Of course, Jesus respected John the Baptist, just as John the Baptist recognized our Lord as God's Messiah. The religious leadership of their day accepted neither. Jesus said:

> "For John came neither eating nor drinking, and they say, 'He has a demon'; the Son of man came eating and drinking, and they say, 'Behold, a glutton and a drunkard, a friend of tax collectors and sinners!' " (Matthew 11:18–19; Luke 7:33–34).

Jesus related to people, and he did not consider the food and drink of wealth to be evil.

Neither did Jesus engage in any self–imposed poverty. He was without wealth, to be sure, and he did not seek it. But he did not deny the value of money. Remember what he said: "Foxes have holes, and birds of the air have nests; but the Son of man has nowhere to lay his head" (Luke 9:58; Matthew 8:20). Some have suggested that Jesus had no home simply because he refused to have the value of personal property and comfort, recognizing them as evil. Hardly! Jesus was involved in serving God and the human family. This service demanded his moving about without roots. In so doing he did not condemn those who were settled in a given place and who had some measure of wealth.

Consider the story of Lazarus the beggar who died and went into what was called "Abraham's bosom" (Luke 16:19–31). This was the equivalent of heaven. On the other hand, the rich man, at whose gate Lazarus lay, died and went into torment. Some have suggested that Lazarus was blessed and went into "Abraham's bosom" simply because he was a poor man and that the rich man went into torment only because he was wealthy. This view is manifestly false since Abraham himself was one of the richest men of his day. Being the patriarch of an extended family, owning large herds, and having freedom to travel were marks of unusual wealth.

Jesus did not consider the possession of material goods to be wrong. Indeed, he recognized the world as being made by God and as the dwelling place of those created by God. To be sure, material possessions should not usurp the place of God. That is idolatry. Rather, they are to be seen as gifts of God and to be used as a stewardship from the Creator.

Fourth, Jesus did not teach that we should maintain a class of poor people. Jesus was in the home of Lazarus whom he had raised from the dead. His sister anointed Jesus' feet with an expensive ointment. But Judas Iscariot was disturbed with this seeming waste and said, "Why was this ointment not sold for three hundred denarii and given to the poor?" (John 12:5). Jesus' answer was instructive: "Let her alone, let her keep it for the day of my burial. The poor you always have with you, but you do not always have me" (John 12:7–8; Mark 14:7; Matthew 26:11). Some have interpreted this statement to mean that Jesus was teaching that it was the will of God that we always have the poor with us. It is obvious, however, that he was simply stating the continuing presence of the poor because he immediately adds, "but you do not always have me." The sale of this expensive ointment would have been some immediate and temporary help for the poor of that day but Jesus indicated that the opportunity of sharing with the poor (see Deuteronomy 15:11) would exist well after his departure.

Poverty is not a blessing, to be sure. Our Lord blessed the poor (Luke 6:20; Matthew 5:3) but as Allan Boesak points out, "poverty is not blessed in the Beatitudes, but the poor."

A more important and obvious fact, however, is that the personal sacrifice and devotion of Mary has continued to inspire people up to our own day. Ruell Howe liked to remind us that God made people to be loved and things to be used. How we reverse God's invention by using people and loving things!

Thus far we have suggested what Jesus did not teach about money. He was not basically an economic theorist; he did not teach that wealth necessarily reflects spiritual blessing and superiority; nor did he teach that wealth is inherently evil; and certainly he did not teach that God wanted an ever-present poorer class in society.

Treasures in Heaven

There is much more that could be pointed out about the teaching of Jesus with respect to money. Indeed, it is surprising how much he said about this subject. He spoke five times more often about earthly possessions, for example, than about prayer.

The primary focus of Jesus' teaching about money is found in the middle of the Sermon on the Mount (Matthew 6:19-34). Here he teaches in essence what is presented in the remainder of the four Gospels concerning this subject.

Jesus presents two wrong relationships with money. These two relationships are the problems of the extremely rich and the extremely poor. The rich may relate to money with greed. Jesus reflects this error in the first portion of this passage:

> "Do not lay up for yourselves treasures on earth, where moth and rust consume and where thieves break in and steal, but lay up for yourselves treasures in heaven, where neither moth nor rust consumes and where thieves do not break in and steal. For where your treasure is, there will your heart be also. The eye is the lamp of the body. So, if your eye is sound, your whole body will be full of light; but if your eye is not sound, your whole body will be full of darkness. If then the light in you is darkness, how great is the darkness! No one can serve two masters; for either he will hate the one and love the other, or he will be devoted to the one and despise the other. You cannot serve God and mammon" (Matthew 6:19-24).

On the other hand, the poor may relate to money with worry. This Jesus describes in the ensuing verses:

> "Therefore I tell you, do not be anxious about your life, what you shall eat or what you shall drink, nor about your body, what you shall put on. Is not life more than food, and the body more than clothing? Look at the birds of the air: they neither sow nor reap nor gather into barns, and yet your heavenly Father feeds them. Are you not of more

value than they? And which of you by being anxious can add one cubit to his span of life? And why are you anxious about clothing? Consider the lilies of the field, how they grow; they neither toil nor spin; yet I tell you, even Solomon in all his glory was not arrayed like one of these. But if God so clothes the grass of the field, which today is alive and tomorrow is thrown into the oven, will he not much more clothe you, O men of little faith? Therefore do not be anxious, saying, 'What shall we eat?' or 'What shall we drink?' or 'What shall we wear?' For the Gentiles seek all these things; and your heavenly Father knows that you need them all. But seek first his kingdom and his righteousness, and all these things shall be yours as well. Therefore do not be anxious about tomorrow, for tomorrow will be anxious for itself. Let the day's own trouble be sufficient for the day" (Matthew 6:25-34).

The Problem with Money—Greed

Greed, on the one hand, is condemned by Jesus for three basic reasons. We should not grasp for money because it is temporal and fading; second, it can become idolatrous, taking the place of—or at least turning us away from—God; third, it can pervert our value systems.

First then, physical and material well-being is temporal and fading. Indeed, it is even faddish. Max Morath points out that in "the ragtime years most people still got around in the horse and buggy—the automobile was considered a plaything of the rich." But now, most of us have cars, so "when you get rich you move out in the country and buy a horse."

At a more serious level Jesus says,

"Do not lay up for yourselves treasures on earth, where moth and rust consume and where thieves break in and steal, but lay up for yourselves treasures in heaven, where neither moth nor rust consumes and where thieves do not break in and steal."

We are, rather, to seek God who supports us eternally.

Second, material wealth can become an idol. Our hearts can be set upon money rather than upon God. John Wesley contended: "When I have any money I get rid of it as quickly as possible, lest it find a way into my heart." "Where your treasure is, there will your heart be also," Jesus said. We commonly and rightly note that our treasure follows our heart. If our hearts are with the poor, our money follows. If our hearts are in missionary endeavors, we give to mission projects. But Jesus' words reverse our expectations. Our hearts follow our treasure, he says. If you see a person scouring the stock market reports, you may be sure that you are observing an investor. Only then do the multitudes of figures create excitement. Our interest follows our money, just as surely as our money follows our interest.

Moreover, we can become slaves to money. We possess material things, but they can come to possess us as well. We normally feel self-sufficient when things are going well. We don't sense our dependence upon God in seasons of sufficiency. As Augustine observed, "God wants to give us something. He cannot, because our hands are full—there's nowhere for Him to put it." We too often call on God as a cosmic lifeguard; we seek not relationship but rescue when we are in over our heads.

It is imperative that we understand our deep need for God. We have been created with what has been called a "God-shaped void" within us. Frederick B. Speakman put it well:

> Someone has imagined God first fashioning man, and one of the hosts of heaven, watching, exclaiming in alarm, but you are giving this creature freedom! He will never be wise enough or strong enough to handle it. He will think himself a god. He will boast in his own self-sufficiency. How can you gamble that he will ever return to you? And God replied, I have left him unfinished within. I have left in him deep needs that only I can satisfy, that out of his desire, his homesickness of soul, he will remember to turn to me.[2]

To not return to God is to fail to see our deepest need. Refusal to turn back to the Creator is to claim no need. That is the essence of idolatry. What is the profit if we have everything that money can represent and lose the One from whom, and for whom, we were made?

This danger of slavery to money is so great that Jesus personalized material wealth by giving it the name "mammon." "No one can serve two masters; for either he will hate the one and love the other, or he will be devoted to the one and despise the other. You cannot serve God and mammon" (Matthew 6:24). If material things drive our experience, we are idolators.

God must be the basic concern of our being. That was the problem of the rich young ruler who approached Jesus. When Jesus told him that he must love his neighbor as himself, the young man claimed that he had kept this and the other commandments of God. Jesus—almost as if to prick this bubble of misunderstanding—told him to sell his goods, give them to the poor, and follow him. The young man would thus show his full devotion to God and neighbor. The rich young man went away sorrowful, we are told, because he had great wealth (Matthew 19:16–22; Mark 10:17–31; Luke 18:18–30). His wealth was more important than his neighbor and more important than God. Again, this view is the essence of idolatry.

Third, material goods can also be perverting. They may be seen as an end rather than as a means. Recall the story which Jesus told about a dishonest steward. He was a rascal and cheated both his master and those with whom he did business. He is not to be commended for these activities, but he was at least wise enough to use money as a means of relating to people. Jesus concluded this strange story with the statement, "And I tell you, make friends for yourselves by means of unrighteous mammon, so that when it fails they may receive you into the eternal habitations" (Luke 16:9).

Money, or mammon, is a means not an end. When money becomes an ultimate goal, our purposes become clouded. We become perverted. We must keep material things as means, not ends. Then we can think within perspective rather than perversion. We can have our vision clarified rather than clouded. If material things become our goals, they become our gods. We are made to relate to God as our ground and goal. To relate significantly to lesser things is idolatrous.

The Problem with Money—Worry

The second half of Jesus' teaching in this section relates to the problem of the poor. This problem is not greed, but unnecessary worry. Jesus teaches that we are to be careful and prudent, not worried and anxious. He further teaches that worry, common as it is, is both harmful and unnecessary. Most important, he points out that worry can be overcome.

The older versions of the Bible called us not to "be careful" about our lives. This translation of "careful" was a good one three hundred years ago. It meant "full of care." But our language has changed. To be full of "care" is to be anxious or worried. Thus, the newer translations (using "anxious") better reflect the meaning of the biblical text (as in Matthew 6:25).

Worrying over the basic necessities of life can be harmful. It can ruin our personal well–being by robbing us of a sense of inner peace. Moreover, it can ruin our activities by misdirecting our energies. So Jesus said, "And which of you by being anxious can add one cubit to his span of life?" (Matthew 6:27).

Worrying won't help you live longer! The fact is that there are some things that we cannot change. The only change which worry brings is a deterioration of life quality through the acid of anxiety.

Moreover, worry is unnecessary, Jesus said. He illustrates this by addressing the two basic necessities of life. We are not to worry about either food or clothing. He compares our need of food with "the birds of the air: they neither sow nor reap nor gather into barns, and yet your heavenly Father feeds them. Are you not of more value than they?" (Matthew 5:26). And he makes worrying about clothing foolish, as it would be for flowers. "Consider the lilies of the field, how they grow; they neither toil nor spin; yet I tell you, even Solomon in all his glory was not arrayed like one of these" (Matthew 6: 28–29). Jesus is not teaching us that we can have everything by doing nothing. Indeed, the birds do seek their food. The important thing is that they don't worry about it. We are to work in constructive activity, but we are not to worry to our detriment and destruction.

Needless worry can be overcome, and it can be overcome positively. We are to seek right relationships. Such a relationship, at the highest level, is with God. "But seek first his kingdom and his righteousness, and all these things shall be yours as well" (Matthew 6:33). Thus we are to be dependent upon God and not worried about the future. After all, we will live! Thoreau noted that we are rich in proportion to the number of things that we can afford to let alone. Relationship with God makes us whole persons. Our earnings are secondary to our relation to God.

This study has led us to see that all of life is for God. Jesus teaches that we are to make God—God's rule and way—central to our concerns. All material things should be secondary. They are important, but they must not usurp the primary importance of God.

And what if we spend more energy and concern on things than on God? Do you feel that you want these ultimate spiritual values—love and relationships rather than just more things—but you admit that you haven't arrived? Good! There is hope if you feel need. Jesus didn't demand that you be perfect. His command was, "Do not be anxious. . . ." Don't be anxious about material things. Don't be anxious about your lack of perfection. He demands desire—a seeking spirit. His command is, "Seek. . . ."

Chapter Five

Did Jesus Allow Divorce?

The Teachings of Jesus Concerning Divorce

—※—

When is a marriage so bad that we can say, "It's best to divorce"? If you were the counselor or pastor in this interview, what would you say?

WOMAN: Well, I always hate to tell other people my troubles. . . . You know, everyone has troubles.

COUNSELOR: But you need to talk to someone.

WOMAN: Well, it's not so much for myself, but the children . . . with Christmas coming so soon and all. . . . They're little you know, and yet, they keep asking when daddy's coming back . . . like everything will be all right then. I shouldn't bother you about it, I know . . . only . . . well, it's happened so often. I'm just running out of excuses for why he isn't home.

COUNSELOR: He goes away quite often?

WOMAN: I never know when he's going next. Things will be all right; he'll work for a while. . . . He never keeps one job for long you know, because as soon as they find out about his gambling, they get suspicious. . . .

COUNSELOR: Does he discuss his gambling habit with his employers?

WOMAN: Oh, he doesn't tell them . . . but someone sees him out at the track, or they'll come by home when he's called in that he is sick. . . . If he's only gone a few days, I can cover up for him, but this time it's been two weeks. It gets worse all the time. The kids are getting older. . . . I don't know what to say to them either . . . don't even know where he is . . . and here it is Christmas, which makes the problem worse. . . . Families are supposed to be together now. . . .

COUNSELOR: Everybody likes to have the family together at Christmas.

WOMAN: Oh, yes. . . . We can't keep on living this way, never knowing when he's going, or when he's coming back. . . . No matter how many bills there are, he never leaves any money. . . . He never thinks of how we feel. . . .

COUNSELOR: He just goes away and lets you take care of yourselves?

WOMAN: He's not mean, understand. . . . He just . . . doesn't seem to think, or to care . . . but when he comes home, he's always so sorry, and we'll think it'll never happen again . . . but it always does. I don't want to think about divorce. I don't want to hate him. . . . It's just that I don't know what to do anymore. . . . Shall I divorce him? Please tell me, what can I do?

Divorce is one of the most divisive issues of our day: It cuts at our most basic social institution. Individual Christians and great denominations differ concerning the propriety of divorce in extreme situations. Basic to the church's response is: What did Jesus teach? The question is far simpler than the answer.

We can ask Jesus questions by approaching what is recorded in the Gospels. If we ask, "When is divorce right?" we face a problem. We ask the question with the assumption that divorce must be right upon some occasions. But Jesus' answer seems to indicate that divorce is never right. If we hear his words on the surface, the response is, "Whoever divorces his wife and marries another, commits adultery against her; and if she divorces her husband and marries another, she commits adultery" (Mark 10:11–12). "When is divorce right?" Jesus' answer seems to be, "Never!"

The fact is, however, that this is too simple a method of determining Jesus' teachings. We ask a question of him in the words and with the background of twentieth-century life. He answers us from within a first-century social situation. He does not answer in terms of our situation. (Indeed, he responds only in view of the ideal will of God, without reference to any cultural contingencies.)

If we are to understand what Jesus would say to us today, we must first understand what he said to the people of his own day. In order to do this, we must understand their situation; then we must understand Jesus' words in that situation. Only after we understand the meaning of his words in the context of two thousand years ago are we in a position to understand what his words say to us today.

An Issue of Righteousness

Let's begin by reconstructing the situation in which Jesus spoke about divorce. We read about his teachings concerning this subject in Mark 10, Luke 16, and in two chapters in Matthew, chapters 5 and 19. We shall direct our primary attention to Matthew for two reasons. First, Matthew recounts Jesus' teachings concerning divorce on two occasions (while Mark and Luke mention them only once). Second, Matthew presents essentially everything that is said in the other two Gospels concerning this subject.

In Matthew, Jesus' words concerning divorce are spoken in situations involving argument. The first of these passages is to be found in chapter 5, beginning with verse 31. The entire last half of the chapter reflects the contrast between Jesus' teachings and the teachings of the religious leaders of his day. "You have heard that it was said to the men of old, 'You shall not kill'. . . . But I say to you that every one who is angry with his brother shall be liable . . ." (Matthew 5:21, 22). These religious leaders were saying that they had not killed anyone; therefore they were righteous. Jesus agreed that they were not murderers, but he would not grant that they were therefore righteous. He seemed to ask, "Have you wanted to kill? Those who hate—those who are angry—cannot claim to be perfectly righteous, even though they may not actually kill."

Similarly, Jesus said,

> "You have heard that it was said, 'You shall not commit adultery.' But I say to you that every one who looks at a woman lustfully has already committed adultery with her in his heart" (Matthew 5:27-28).

Again, the religious leaders would say, "We have not committed adultery; therefore we are righteous." But Jesus would only admit that they were not technical adulterers; he would not grant that they were therefore perfectly righteous. Genuine righteousness reflects not only our acts, but our desires. Jesus seemed to ask, "But have you *wanted* to commit adultery?"

It is in this context that Jesus mentions divorce. He goes on to say,

> "It was also said, 'Whoever divorces his wife, let him give her a certificate of divorce.' But I say to you that every one who divorces his wife, except on the ground of unchastity, makes her an adulteress; and whoever marries a divorced woman commits adultery" (Matthew 5:31–32).

The religious leaders would say, "We have only divorced our wives according to the rules. In every instance we gave a certificate of divorce. Therefore we are righteous." Again Jesus would respond, "Never; you are only those who have kept the rule about giving a certificate of divorce. This does not make you righteous." Indeed, he said, "But I say to you that every one who divorces his wife, except on the ground of unchastity, makes her an adulteress." That is, the divorcing husband forces his wife into the compromising situation of remarriage to another man. He continued: "And whoever marries a divorced woman commits adultery." That is, by divorcing the wife, the husband may affect a third party who is now uninvolved and who may later marry the divorced wife.

Thus, Jesus said that one cannot claim to be righteous when he dissolves a marriage for inadequate reason. He is not only wrong in this particular action, but is responsible for the future actions of his wife because of the situation into which he has forced her.

Notice that there is no word concerning the wife divorcing her husband. In the Jewish society of those days marriage and divorce were initiated by men only. Roman society was more lax. Seneca wrote that women were married to be divorced in order to be married. In Rome, he said, women dated the years by the names of their husbands! Juvenal chides a woman for having eight husbands in five autumns. Greco–Roman society was not constrained by biblical insights. The great orator Demosthenes said, "We have courtesans for the sake of pleasure; we have concubines for the sake of daily cohabitation; we have wives for the purpose of having children legitimately, and of having a faithful guardian for all our household affairs."[1]

Although Jewish society generally held women in higher regard than the society of the Greeks or the Romans, marriage remained a personal relationship, not a civil or religious one. A couple was married in that society under circumstances far different from those of our own day. It was not a matter of both parties saying, "I do," and the minister, priest, or rabbi pronouncing them husband and wife. Marriage was a matter of the man saying, "I take thee to wife after the manner of the sons of Israel." It was basically a personal action on the part of a man. The woman was passive. The marriage was not a civil ceremony recorded in the county seat, nor was it a religious ceremony recorded in the annals of the church or synagogue. Thus it is not strange to find that divorce was a similarly personal matter. The man did not have to seek out a rabbi or a judge. He could simply dismiss his wife and he was divorced.

A single check was put on the right of a man to divorce his wife easily and hastily. This was the requirement of Moses that he write out a certificate of divorce, give it to her, and officially send her out of his house (Deuteronomy 24:1). The certificate was necessary for her protection, of course, since the man could send her out in a quick fit of anger and later claim he was only kidding! She would never know if she was actually divorced or simply enduring one of his tantrums.

Jesus goes further by saying that the certificate did not make the procedure right. On the contrary, a man should love his wife, and they should remain one for life. The fact that he had kept the rule of writing a bill of divorce did not make him either a righteous man or a loving husband. Far from it!

The Letter of the Law

The other passage in Matthew which reflects Jesus' teachings concerning divorce is in chapter 19. Here is an actual encounter of Jesus with the religious leaders of his day. They asked him, "Is it lawful to divorce one's wife for any cause?" (Matthew 19:36). This was an extremely significant question. If religious persons of that day wanted to determine the cause for which they could divorce, they would have to look at the Scriptures. There is only one passage that told men how to give a divorce. The first verse in Deuteronomy 24 reads, "When a man takes a wife and marries her, if then she finds no favor in his eyes because he has found some indecency in her, and he writes her a bill of divorce and puts it in her hand and sends her out of his house. . . ." The religious leaders read this passage and asked, "Now what are the appropriate bases for divorce in this verse?" The answer, of course, was thought to be in the words, "if then she finds no favor in his eyes because he has found some indecency in her." What does this mean? Well, we know what it meant in Jesus' day.

The teachings of the religious leaders of Jesus' day are collected in what is called *Mishna*. There we may find the interpretation of this verse. Note a significant passage:

> The School of Shammai says: A man may not divorce his wife unless he has found unchastity in her, for it is written, because he has found in her indecency in something. And the School of Hillel says: He may divorce her, even if she spoiled a dish for him, for it is written, because he has found in her indecency in something. Rabbi Akiba says: Even if he found another fairer than she, for it is written, and it shall be if she finds no favor in his eyes. . . .[2]

Three views concerning the possible bases of divorce according to Deuteronomy 24:1 are thus presented. First, Shammai, a great rabbi, taught that one could divorce his wife only if she was unfaithful.

The second view was expounded by Hillel, who was an even more respected religious teacher than Shammai. Hillel taught that a man could divorce his wife for just about any cause, even "if she spoiled a dish for him." If she spoiled the soup or prepared some meat with the wrong sauce, she could be divorced. Simply write her a certificate!

This view is reflective of the American bridegroom who awakened his wife holding a bed–tray with a glass of fresh orange juice, fried eggs, crisp bacon, toast, and coffee. "See what I've done?" asked the bridegroom. "Every single thing you darling boy," she cooed. "Good," he grunted, "that's the way I want it every morning!"

The third position, taught by Rabbi Akiba, went even further. He said that if you saw another woman who was more beautiful than your wife, then you could give your wife a divorce. After all, he claimed, that's what the Bible says—"if she finds no favor in his eyes. . . ."

Now we can see what was meant by the question of the Pharisees to Jesus: "Is it lawful to divorce one's wife *for any cause?*" (author's emphasis). In other words, they wanted to know if Jesus agreed with Hillel and Akiba that husbands may divorce their wives for preparing the wrong meal or because they had seen someone more beautiful!

This was the situation in which Jesus made his statement concerning divorce. The assumption was that a woman could not divorce her husband under any circumstance. On the other hand, the husband could divorce his wife for any reason. And it was not difficult. All he had to do was to put it in writing. Marriage was losing its definition as a deep relationship of a continuing nature. It was just something to be maintained as long as the excitement, the zip, the pleasure of relationship was there for the man. If that began to wear thin, he could simply evict her.

This description sounds like some of our current concepts of marriage! Yet we must recall that marriages of long ago were not built upon extended courtships. They were determined and arranged by parents and felt to be useful only as long as the relationship was of value to the man.

At the other extreme, we put marriage at the level of a perennially adolescent excitement. When the "romance" wears off, then perhaps we shall get a divorce. When Jack Carter was married, he remembered George Burns approaching him at the reception and asking, "Is this your third marriage?" "Yes," Carter answered. Burns said, "Good, keep trying until you get it right!"

Ilka Chase has told of the aftermath of her divorce from Louis Calhern, an internationally famous character actor. His next wife was Julia Hoyt. Miss Chase, going through a trunk, found a box of handsomely engraved cards, bearing simply the name of Mrs. Louis Calhern. Feeling it a shame they should go to waste, she wrapped and sent them to her successor with a little note, "Dear Julia, I hope these reach you in time!"

When the Pharisees argued with Jesus concerning divorce, their question was, "Is it lawful to divorce one's wife for any cause?" (Matthew 19:3). We note that they put the question as being essentially a legal matter. Is it *lawful*? We also see that they were asking whether he agreed with Shammai, who taught that one could divorce his wife only on the basis of unfaithfulness, or with Hillel, who taught that a husband could divorce his wife "for *any* cause."

Marriage as Intended by God

Jesus does not give a direct reply to the Pharisees' question. They wanted him to say either yes or no, but he answered at a deeper level, relating to the better motivations of men. This response is clearly in line with the deeply religious and idealistic teachings of Jesus. He is not interested in the legality of the issue—with the way we would make people live. He is rather interested in our seeking to do the will of God—with our learning how we ought to live. Jesus is not interested in the legal requirements of the case, but with the deep moral commitments of the one who desires to do the will of God. Moral obligations before God will, obviously, be higher than any simple legal requirements.

Thus we find that Jesus turns away from the Old Testament passage that allows divorce. He rather goes back to the basis of marriage as originally given by God. He moves back from the book of Deuteronomy to the book of Genesis. He answered,

"Have you not read that he who made them from the beginning made them male and female, and said, 'For this reason a man shall leave his father and mother and be joined to his wife, and the two shall become one flesh'? So they are no longer two but one flesh. What therefore God has joined together, let not man put asunder" (Matthew 19:4–6; Genesis 1:27; 2:24).

It is obvious that Jesus is going far beyond any legal demands. He is interested in the ultimate will of God. Jesus asks about the ideal marriage relationship rather than about the technicalities which allow a breaking of the marriage relationship.

This ideal perception of marriage was reflected in the simple eloquence of the seventeenth–century biblical commentator Matthew Henry writing of the creation of woman from the side of man. She was, wrote Henry, "not made out of his head to rule over him, nor out of his feet to be trampled upon by him; but out of his side to be equal with him; under his arm to be protected; and near his heart to be loved."[3]

In our generation the ideal marriage has been described well by Louis Anspacher: "Marriage is that relationship between man and woman in which the independence is equal, the dependence mutual, and the obligation reciprocal."

When Jesus argued with his legalistic antagonists, they asked, "Why then did Moses command one to give a certificate of divorce, and to put her away?" (Matthew 19:7). Since Jesus had claimed that it was the will of God that no one separate a couple whom God had joined, they rebutted that Moses commanded one to give a certificate of divorce. Jesus responded that Moses never commanded any such thing. He only made an allowance for what was already being done, and added a requirement that would help curb excesses. The words of Jesus were, "For your hardness of heart Moses allowed you to divorce your wives, but from the beginning it was not so" (Matthew 19:8).

It is interesting to note that the men arguing with Jesus considered these words of Moses a command. His directive dealt only with a big *if.* If a man is to divorce his wife and send her away, then he must write her a bill of divorce. Moses never said that a man should send his wife away, and then write her a bill of divorce.

Moses' concern was that a woman be protected with a written document in the event that a man sent her away.

Jesus refused to speak of a commandment and said, "Moses allowed you to divorce your wives," but only because of "hardness of heart." Moses knew that husbands were putting away their wives. He just wanted them to get a decent break in the midst of an evil situation.

But in the light of the ideal view of marriage, there is no room for divorce. Thus, Jesus went on to say, "whoever divorces his wife, except for unchastity, and marries another, commits adultery" (Matthew 19:9).

In summary we may note that teachers of Jesus' day had a running controversy over divorce. Jesus refused to take a specific side in this controversy. Rather, he lifted the discussion above divorce to uphold the original institution of marriage. God had made man and woman to become one in marriage. The divine intention was that, once married, they should not be divided. Jesus was not interested in any possibilities of avoiding God's ideal purpose which might be allowed in the law. He was rather interested in determining what the law really meant, what it ought to be, and, ultimately, what was the actual will of God. The regulation of Deuteronomy was a compromise between the ideal will of God and the inability of sinful men to maintain these ideals. But Jesus knew and knows nothing of the laxity that is born of compromise. He jumps over the compromise of the legalist in favor of the original ideal of God.

Notice that Jesus' teachings assume a desire to know and to do the will of God. Jesus desires of us this ultimate devotion to God and God's purposes, and he speaks of human relationships, including marriage, within this context. A couple should remain united— not because they are always as romantic and excited as teenagers on their first date nor because it is a rigid rule that they must not break—because this permanent, loving relationship is best for us. It is best for our families, for society at large, and for our relationships with those who may see our devotion to God.

In the crucible of daily experience a good marriage requires the determination of both wife and husband. True love involves a stubborn commitment. The marriage vows include the "worse" as well as the "better." The road of a solid marriage is sometimes smooth, often rough and rocky, but always interesting.

Other questions concerning divorce remain. We can see that Jesus spoke to people who claimed to do the will of God, while they did things that were obviously immoral and self-centered. We note that he was interested in upholding the ultimate will of God to those people. We observe that he answered their arguments by which they endeavored to lower the purposes of God to their own legal demands. But the questions remain.

What Is the Answer?

Consider the woman in counseling at the opening of this chapter. Does Jesus answer her question? Should she get a divorce? Jesus does not clearly answer her question, because he does not speak to this particular problem. Does this mean that the teachings of Jesus are irrelevant to her problem? Not at all. Jesus speaks deeply to her concern and need—deeply, but not specifically. He does not give a direct answer as to whether or not she should get a divorce in this specific situation. He speaks instead to her sense of worth as a person. He speaks to her sense of love for God, her family, and her husband. He speaks to her sense of perseverance and sacrificial giving in the midst of an almost overwhelming situation. He speaks—and stands beside her.

There are other questions. Should divorcees remarry? Jesus does not answer this question specifically either. He is, rather, interested in the ideal will of God. The ideal is that individuals not become divorced persons.

Does this mean, then, that Jesus is unconcerned about people who have not met the ideal will of God? Absolutely not! Nothing could be more foreign to the life or teachings of Jesus Christ. He "came to seek and to save the lost" (Luke 19:10). He came not for the healthy, but for the sick. He came not only to describe the ideal of God, but also to redeem those who acknowledge that they fell short of that ideal.

It is essential that we embody the message of redemption and forgiveness in our day. Paul Tournier recalls an experience of this redemptive forgiveness:

During our cruise to the North Cape last year I was leaning on the rail one day watching the wonderful Norwegian landscape slip by, with its incredibly green islands and shores contrasting with the great glaciers which come down almost to the sea. A doctor passed in silence, and stood leaning against the same rail beside me, studying the same spectacle. After a moment or two he said, "I'm quite upset. I have just been told that one of our colleagues here has been divorced and remarried. Is that true?" "Yes," I said. After a further silence he went on, "How is that possible? How can you agree to his taking his place among us Christian doctors?"

I said nothing for the moment. Then my friend added, "Do you not believe that divorce is disobedience to God? A sin?"—"Certainly," I said, "but if we could have only sinless men among us, there would be no one here; at any rate, I should not be here. We are all alike, we are all forgiven sinners." A long silence followed. My friend went away. Later he returned. "You are right," he said briefly. "Now I know what grace means."

There you are; he is a zealous Christian, whom I like and esteem highly, very sincere, very reasonable with his faith, keen in evangelizing and in no way pharisaical. The Church proclaims the grace of God. And moralism, which is the negation of it, always creeps into its bosom, most particularly among those people who have the most praiseworthy care to uphold their faith by the rectitude of their moral conduct.[4]

Jesus faced a woman who was not only divorced but who was an adulteress. Did he reject her? No! She was rejected by the people who were so intent upon getting their divorces legally. But Jesus pointed out the sin of all those others. There they stood with hatred in their eyes, their guilt projected upon a helpless woman. There they were, holding large rocks, ready to crush her face and body as they brought this sinner to death. Jesus simply said, "Let him who is without sin among you be the first to throw a stone at her" (John 8:7).

There was another woman who was known to be a sinner within the community. But she found one truly good person—a man who reflected more than any other what God was really like—and found that he loved her as a person, a human being created by God. In her devotion, she wept at his feet. Jesus said to her, "I tell you, her sins, which are many, are forgiven, for she loved much; but he who is forgiven little, loves little" (Luke 7:47).

There are many areas of our lives that are not right. There are things about us that cannot stand the scrutiny of almighty God. But we can be—indeed we are—uplifted by the love of Jesus Christ for us even in our sin. Have you felt inadequate before God? Have you felt that you are not good enough to stand comparison with Jesus Christ? Have you felt this sense of personal unworthiness along with a sense of personal guilt? Then you are either in or close to the kingdom. Jesus came to teach us about the ideal purposes of God. He came also to bring us into an ideal personal relationship with God. He perfectly presented the teachings of God. He perfectly reflected what God is like. He also fully met and continues to meet our needs in making us children of God.

Chapter Six

The Son of God?

The Teachings of Jesus Concerning Himself

Have you wondered what Jesus was really like? Perhaps your thinking is like that of one of these students:

JIM: Hi Earl. Sit down, we're talking about the lecture we just came from . . . Dr. Johnson's.

EARL: Yeah. . . . Did you notice that one thing he said? . . . It bothered me a little bit. Remember he was listing the great men of history and he mentioned Jesus Christ? . . . I didn't think it fit!

JOAN: What's wrong with that?

EARL: He wasn't a man. . . . He was God!

JIM: Well, I have to disagree; I can grant that Jesus was a great man, but he certainly wasn't God.

JOAN: I'm not really in agreement with either of you. I think he was probably the greatest man in history, and . . . well, he is still God; I think that's what he claimed himself.

EARL: Well, how can you be God *and* man at the same time?

JIM: Seems you've got a little problem there, Joan!

JOAN: I just know that's what he claimed. And that's what his followers thought.

Was he the son of God—really? Was Jesus divine? Did he claim to be God? Was he only a man?

The Great Offense

These students didn't recognize it, but they were talking about Christmas. Christmas is a joy. It is also an offense. It is a joy because it is the season in which gifts are exchanged and children are central. It is an offense, because it is the time when Christians claim that God became human. There are many who feel that this belief is pure foolishness. They believe that God is in heaven, but has nothing to do with our world. Christmas is a nice story, but there is no factual basis in it. God does not become human.

Christians and Christianity are also offenses. A Christian is, by definition, one who takes the meaning of Christmas seriously. God did become human. Jesus Christ is the Son of God. This conviction is common to all Christian groups. The National Council of the Churches of Christ has a brief statement of doctrine as its basis of membership. The primary focus of this statement is the recognition of Jesus Christ as "the incarnate Word of God, as Savior and Lord." The World Council of Churches has a statement that is even more offensive to the non-Christian mind. It confesses "the Lord Jesus Christ as God and Savior." The Roman Catholic Church, which is not included in the National Council of the Churches of Christ or the World Council of Churches, also holds that Jesus Christ is the Son of God. Many other Christian groups which do not fellowship through the ecumenical movement hold this same teaching. The belief that Jesus is divine is basic to being a Christian.

Christianity has much in common with other religions. Historically, the Christian faith is related most closely to Judaism and Islam. These three faiths affirm the Hebrew Bible as inspired and authoritative Scripture. It is no accident that people have seen "Allah" of Islam and "the Lord" of Judaism to be closely related to, or even identified with, the God and Father of our Lord Jesus Christ.

But Moslems and Jews alike have rejected vehemently the claims of Christianity. This rejection is, basically, because of the Christmas story—that God took on human form. Many people simply will not accept Jesus Christ as the Son of God.

The offense of Christianity's central teaching is not something new. It was a stumbling block in the early church as well. The apostle Paul found that the preaching of Jesus Christ as God's Son and the world's Savior was rejected both by the Jews and the Greeks. He wrote to the Christians in Corinth saying: "For Jews demand signs and Greeks seek wisdom, but we preach Christ crucified, a stumbling block to Jews and folly to Gentiles, but to those who are called, both Jews and Greeks, Christ the power of God and the wisdom of God" (1 Corinthians 1:22–24).

Jews have much in common with Christians. Religious Jews and Christians alike believe that God has acted in history in times past. Jews and Christians alike believe that God forgives sins, and that we all need forgiveness. But the radical sense of human beings as sinners and rebels against God is a Christian understanding. Christians feel that we have violated God's intentions even to the point of necessitating the death of God's Son. The deep awareness of sin and of the limitless love of God who forgives sin in the sacrifice of the eternal Word is an offense to the Jewish mind. To many it is blasphemy. In the words of Paul, "We preach Christ crucified, a stumbling block to Jews."

By the same token, the cross was foolishness to the philosophically oriented Greek mind. When Paul would preach Christ as the Savior of the world to a Greek audience, there were those who would say, "Oh, come now, Paul, get off it. You're not going to tell us that a crucified Jew was really the Son of God. You can't convince us that Jesus' death is the way God comes to meet us and relate us with the divine. This is pure foolishness." The Greeks sought wisdom, but they heard a message of Christ crucified. To them it was folly.

Soren Kierkegaard, Emil Brunner, Karl Barth, and other theologians have emphasized that we are offended by Jesus Christ. We are offended that any human being could make such great demands upon us. Who can tell us that we should pray for our enemies or that we should sell our possessions and give to the poor? We are offended further that Jesus should claim to be the Son of God. Perhaps someone else could, but not Jesus! He was from a minority group, from the lower social strata, and without sophistication. We find it particularly offensive that the Son of God should hang on a cross at the city dump with flies gathering on his bleeding body. We do not expect the ultimate revelation of God to be seen this way.

The message of God on a cross is particularly unacceptable to many of the current generation. There are those in our society who view God as a caricature. They see God as a bloodthirsty deity who demands a sacrifice. (Some have said that this is Paul's fault. They claim that Jesus never presented this view of God; Jesus never claimed to be the Son of God. To such people Paul and the other apostles become the villains in the story of the early Christian church.)

This modern reaction against the cross, like the ancient reaction of the Jews and Greeks who rejected the preaching of the apostles, fails to account for the deep personal concern of the Christian God. We are loved genuinely by God—even in our sin. We are not simply functioning units who need repairing—either psychologically or physically. We are not simply individuals who contribute to the welfare of the State or the corporate social structure and who therefore can be lost in the masses. We are, rather, persons who have been made and loved by God. We are persons who have, in our independence and waywardness, rebelled against our loving Maker. We are sinners who have been cut off from fellowship with God. It is in the context of personal love that judgment and punishment are not to be seen as something evil. Because God loves us as persons Jesus Christ comes to absorb our guilt and judgment. He thus reveals what God is really like, and reestablishes our personal relationship with God and with one another. This good news meets our deepest needs. Consider the witness of Joni Eareckson, who is totally paralyzed from the neck down. Following her graduation as "Most Athletic Girl" at a Baltimore high school, she broke her neck in a 1967 diving accident. How has she responded to this catastrophe?

Somebody has to bathe me and brush my hair and feed me. In a sense, success for me is just getting up in the morning, looking at that wheelchair and saying, 'Yeah, it's still here.' . . . God began his earthly existence in a stinky stable. He got angry. He was lonely. He went without a place to call his own, abandoned by his closest friends. He wept real tears. This is a God I can trust. I know my tears count with him.[1]

Joni Eareckson's life is one of ongoing pain. But her commitment to Christ delivers her from complaint. She rejoices in the conviction that the One crucified but living meets her daily needs.

God's Equal

Our question is: Was Jesus divine? If we are to put this question into proper perspective, we must review the earliest Christian records of Jesus—the New Testament. There is no question concerning the New Testament teachings about Jesus. He was clearly divine. The two writers of the New Testament who make this most obvious are Paul and John.

The apostle Paul wrote a letter to the church in Colossae, a group of Christians whom he had never seen. These people were bothered by some teachers who were indicating that Jesus was not really God. Paul reacted by emphasizing—and thereby giving us the New Testament teaching—that Jesus is clearly divine. Consider just three verses of Paul's letter to these Colossian Christians. Professor F. F. Bruce, retired from the University of Manchester, translates them in these words:

> This Redeemer of ours is the very image of God whom none can see; He is the Firstborn, prior to all creation and superior over it, because it was through Him that the universe was created. Yes, all things in heaven and on earth, visible things and things invisible, whether thrones or dominions or principalities or powers—they have all been created through Him and for Him. He Himself existed before them all, and it is through Him that everything holds together (Colossians 1:15-17).[2]

It is obvious that Paul is presenting Jesus as divine. He is the creator of all things. He existed before anything else, and he sustains the universe.

Jean Paul Richter presses the same claim in modern terms: "Christ who, being the holiest among the mighty and the mightiest among the holy, lifted with His pierced hands empires off their hinges and turned the stream of centuries out of its channel, he still governs the ages."

Similarly, Paul wrote to the Christians at Philippi. As opposed to the church in Colossae, Paul was intensely familiar with these Christians. Indeed, this was the church toward which he seemed to show the greatest affection. In the second chapter of his letter to the Philippian Christians, Paul encouraged a sense of humility. He said that Jesus showed the greatest humility by giving up his divine rights in order to serve us. These verses make this point.

> Let your attitude be that of Christ Jesus Himself. For he, who had always been God by nature, did not cling to his privileges as God's equal, but stripped himself of every advantage by consenting to be a slave by nature and being born a man (Philippians 2:5–7 Phillips).

Paul also says that Jesus had certain prerogatives as God's equal, but he gave up these prerogatives in his desire to rescue those whom he loved. How would Paul answer our question, "Was Jesus divine?"—With an emphatic yes!

John, similarly, held that Jesus was deity. He begins his Gospel with the words: "In the beginning was the Word, and the Word was with God, and the Word was God. He was in the beginning with God; all things were made through him, and without him was not anything made that was made" (John 1:1–3). John used the term "word" to describe Jesus in this passage. Word was a familiar term to many of the philosophical teachers of John's day and before. They saw the Word as an eternal, rational principle which sustained the rational universe. In describing Jesus as the Word, John presented him as an eternal and divine person; and, indeed, he was of the very essence of God.

C. S. Lewis presented this incarnation graphically:

> The Eternal Being, who knows everything and who created the whole universe, became not only a man but (before that) a baby, and before that a fetus inside a woman's body. If you want to get the hang of it, think how you would like to become a slug or a crab.[3]

John's Gospel begins by holding Jesus to be divine. There is hardly a chapter thereafter that does not underscore this teaching. "I and the Father are one" (John 10:30). "[I pray] . . . that they may all be one; even as thou, Father, art in me, and I in thee, that they also may be in us, so that the world may believe that thou has sent me" (17:21). There is little question that Jesus is reflected here as the eternal Son of God.

Paul and John are joined by other New Testament writers in recognizing Jesus as the Son of God:

> All except Matthew, Mark, Titus, and the Johannine Epistles style Jesus 'Lord'; and the excepted writings all use comparable, if not even more significant terms—'Son of God', or 'Saviour' . . . with few exceptions, they are Jewish writings, or, without any exception, monotheistic. This only makes it more remarkable that, strictly maintaining their monotheism and without the slightest concession in this respect to pagan thought, they all adopt this attitude of reverence for Jesus.[4]

There is no question that the writers of the New Testament saw Jesus as divine. Indeed, there is no question that the early Christians knew Jesus to be the Son of God. We should, however, recognize the possibility that they were all wrong. Could not Jesus have understood himself to be a mere man? And could not the early Christians have misconstrued his teaching completely? How can we be sure of the teaching of Jesus as to whether or not he was divine?

If we are to know the basic thinking of Jesus, we must go back to the earliest records of his teaching. These accounts are to be found in the first three Gospels—Matthew, Mark, and Luke. We have thousands of handwritten copies of these original Gospels from the early centuries of the Christian era. Scholars have determined what was actually written in those original manuscripts, as well as what changes later copyists introduced. Moreover, scholars have evaluated the similarities and differences of these Gospels critically.

Certain general conclusions have become obvious to the world of biblical scholarship. First, the earliest Gospel to be written was Mark. Second, Matthew and Luke both made use of Mark as they wrote their Gospels. Third, Matthew and Luke also had another source apart from Mark that they both used. Beyond that, Matthew and Luke each had access to particular sources. These facts bring us back to an ability to point to the earliest records of Jesus' teaching, records that were written while many of the eyewitnesses of Jesus' life were still living.

What do these earliest records reflect about Jesus' teachings concerning himself? The interpretations of Paul, John, Peter, and the other early Christian leaders aside, what do our earliest sources teach us concerning Jesus' own claims? Was he divine?

Scholars have determined that the best way to get at Jesus' understanding of himself as seen in the Gospels is through his names and claims, through his appellations and assumptions.[5] Jesus used many names in referring to himself. (He normally did not refer to himself with the personal pronoun "I.") He gave descriptions and made claims about himself as related to others. Let us consider first the names or titles which Jesus used for himself. Then we will examine his general assumptions and specific claims.

The Names of Jesus

Jesus speaks of himself in many terms, including Son of man; Son of God; Messiah; Lord; Master; Son of David; Servant; Shepherd; the true vine; the bread of life; the door of the sheep; the resurrection and the life; the way, the truth, and the life; the amen, among others. There are three names that stand out most commonly. These are the Son of God, the Son of man, and Messiah.

Son of God

First, consider Jesus' use of the term "Son of God." When he was only twelve, he addressed his mother, saying, "Did you not know that I must be in my Father's house?" (Luke 2:49). Since Jesus spoke so commonly of God as his Father, this is tantamount to calling himself the Son of God.

There are clearer claims than this in the earliest written source, the Gospel according to Mark. The early verses of chapter 12 reflect a story which Jesus told about a man who had planted a vineyard and who had left workmen to care for it. When the owner sent a servant to collect his share of the yield, the workmen beat the servant and sent him away. They similarly beat and even killed servants who were subsequently sent. He continued by saying,

"He had still one other, a beloved son; finally he sent him to them saying, 'They will respect my son.' But those tenants said to one another, 'This is the heir; let us kill him, and the inheritance will be ours.' And they took him and killed him. . . ." (Mark 12:6–8).

This story points to Jesus himself as this "beloved son" and "the heir."

Jesus again referred to himself as God's Son in the next chapter, Mark 13. When Jesus spoke of the activities of God in the distant future, he concluded by saying, "But of that day or that hour no one knows, not even the angels in heaven, nor the Son, but only the Father" (Mark 13:32). He indicated an ascending order from angels to God. The fact that he put himself between the angels and God means that he claimed a position higher than the angels and made himself subject only to God.

We have observed that biblical scholars have recognized that Matthew and Luke had an earlier source apart from Mark. There are verses that reflect words written earlier than any of those of the apostle Paul or John or any other writers of the New Testament. Yet they present Jesus as making a claim of relationship to God as Son that is as great as any found in the New Testament. Jesus said, "All things have been delivered to me by my Father; and no one knows the Son except the Father, and no one knows the Father except the Son and any one to whom the Son chooses to reveal him" (Matthew 11:27; Luke 10:22). Interpreters recognize this as Jesus' highest claim to divinity. They also recognize that this verse is unquestionably authentic. No critical attempt at undermining these words has been successful. In the earliest sources, Jesus clearly claimed to be the Son of God.

Son of Man

Jesus also claimed to be the "Son of man." We often think of this second title as being the opposite of Son of God. We assume that Son of God refers to Jesus' divinity, whereas Son of man emphasizes his humanity.

We are correct in seeing Jesus as both God and man. We are wrong in thinking that the term Son of man means humanity. If we are to understand what Jesus meant by this most common designation of himself, we must see the background out of which he used this term. This background is the Hebrew Bible. The most significant passage for our understanding is in the seventh chapter of Daniel:

> I saw in the night visions,
> and behold, with the clouds of heaven
>   there came one like a son of man,
> and he came to the Ancient of Days
>   and was presented before him.
> And to him was given dominion
>   and glory and kingdom,
> that all peoples, nations, and languages
>   should serve him;
> his dominion is an everlasting dominion,
>   which shall not pass away,
>   and his kingdom one
>   that shall not be destroyed.
> —Daniel 7:13–14

Jesus uses the term Son of man to speak of himself as God's Son—as the one who will ultimately be Lord of all—when he stands before the Jewish high priest in Mark's Gospel.

> . . . the high priest asked him, "Are you the Christ, the Son of the Blessed?" And Jesus said, "I am; and you will see the Son of man seated at the right hand of Power, and coming with the clouds of heaven." And the high priest tore his garments, and said, "Why do we still need witnesses? You have heard his blasphemy" (Mark 14:61–64).

Here we note that Jesus is asked specifically if he is the Son of God and the Christ. He answers that he is. Then Jesus speaks of himself as the Son of man who will come on clouds of heaven and who will sit at the right hand of God. It is obvious, then, that Jesus refers to himself as the Son of man in the sense of his elevation and unique relationship to God. The title reflects his divinity, sovereignty, and eternal power more than it does his relationship with humanity.

Messiah

The passage to which we have just referred (Mark 14:61–64)

presents the high priest asking Jesus if he was the "Messiah." This is the third significant title that refers to Jesus in the Gospels. We often speak of Jesus by the name Jesus Christ. Because Christ is so often related to the name Jesus, some assume that Christ is Jesus' surname. Christ is not a name at all, however, but a title. It means Messiah. The Messiah is the "anointed one" whom the Jewish people expected to come as a deliverer. When we speak of Jesus Christ we mean Jesus the Christ, that is, Jesus the Messiah. When Jesus was on trial before the high priest, he was asked specifically, "Are you the Christ, the Son of the Blessed?" Jesus accepted this title and responded directly, "I am." The claim of the title of Messiah is in the earliest record of Jesus' words about himself.

Jesus is understood to be the Messiah implicitly in many portions of the Gospels. This was true at his baptism and temptation as well as at that climactic point in which Peter recognized him as the Messiah: "You are the Christ, the Son of the living God" (Matthew 16:16; Mark 8:29; Luke 9:20).

It is clear that Jesus claimed these divine titles for himself. He claimed to be the Son of God, the Son of man, and the Messiah who would deliver God's people.

The Claims of Jesus

Jesus also made certain assumptions that constitute claims to divinity. Probably the most striking of these is his claim to our absolute devotion. Referring to Mark, we find that Jesus assumes the right to our total commitment.

> "If any man would come after me, let him deny himself and take up his cross and follow me. For whoever would save his life will lose it; and whoever loses his life for my sake and the gospel's will save it. . . . For whoever is ashamed of me and my words in this adulterous and sinful generation, of him will the Son of man also be ashamed, when he comes in the glory of his Father with the holy angels" (Mark 8:34–35, 38).

The minister of the gospel, indeed every Christian witness, makes similar assumptions when ministering in Christ's name. Dr. Gene Bartlett describes this assumption as it was reflected in his early ministry:

When I was a student in the theological school, I spent a weekend with friends at a lakeside home where Dr. Justin Wroe Nixon, a distinguished teacher and preacher, was also a guest. Because he was suffering from laryngitis, Dr. Nixon had to carry on a conversation by writing on a pad! In this interesting way we began to talk about theology, particularly as it related to pastoral experience, for I had just started in a village church.

At one point Dr. Nixon wrote on his pad the question, 'How do you think of Jesus?' Then he listed some alternatives: 'As a social prophet? As a teacher? As God?' I said that my whole feeling about Jesus had taken on new dimensions since I began my pastoral responsibilities. When I visited a hospital, I thought of Jesus' healing. When I sat with a troubled person, I remembered how he reached out and brought calm. Where there was bereavement, I remembered his times of comforting. In short, he had become far more real as I faced actual human situations. Jesus Christ was somehow present to us. At this, Dr. Nixon took his pencil and on his pad checked, 'as God.'

Now, a lifetime of ministry later, that conviction is stronger than ever.[6]

Jesus also makes other assumptions. He assumes the right to forgive sins. He further assumes the right to speak with an authority that could only come from God. His emphatic use of the pronoun "I" would reflect a terrible conceit if it came from any other lips.

In summary, we have seen that the early Christians saw Jesus as the Son of God. Our concern has also been to see what Jesus thought of his relationship to God. We find that he made a clear claim to be the Son of God. He did so by using and accepting titles that showed his divinity and by assuming a special relationship with God.

We cannot just leave the issue of Jesus' identity there, however. Jesus' claims also confront us. He came as God's Son to meet us in our need. Once he confronts us, we cannot ignore him. His claim, and my assumption as a Christian, is that he confronts every person.

You can deny Jesus Christ, but you cannot ignore him. He is there. He claims to be divine. He claims to have authority over our experience. Thus, we are driven back to a trilemma which has been noted on many occasions. Either Jesus was a deceiver, or he was deluded, or he was divine. We can say he was lying. He was a deceiver. We can pass him off quickly as not possessing all his faculties. He was deluded. But if we don't see him as deceiving or deluded, we must recognize his divinity.

C. S. Lewis has presented the problem most eloquently:

> I am trying here to prevent anyone saying the really foolish thing that people often say about Him: "I'm ready to accept Jesus as a great moral teacher, but I don't accept His claim to be God." That is the one thing we must not say. A man who is merely a man and said the sort of things Jesus said would not be a great moral teacher. He would either be a lunatic—on the level with a man who says he is a poached egg—or else he would be the Devil of Hell. You must make your choice. Either this man was, and is, the Son of God or else a madman or something worse.[7]

When we are convinced that Jesus is the Son of God, the gospel calls us to decision. The decision is more than a rational one. It is a deeply personal and wholistic commitment. In one of his speeches, E. Stanley Jones described an extensive interview with Mahatma Gandhi. As the conversation drew to a close, Gandhi demanded, "Tell me in one sentence what Christ means to you." Jones recalled that he was shocked under the impact of the question, but answered reverently: "All I want and need of God, that Jesus Christ my Lord, is to me."

Chapter Seven

Why Do We Suffer?

The Teachings of Jesus Concerning Human Suffering

—✺—

W hy does God allow sickness, suffering, pain? The question is not new to philosophers and theologians. To make the matter personal—Why did this happen to me? This question is not new to any of us. How many times have you wondered why God should allow that particular problem to become yours?

We can recognize some value that comes from suffering and pain. In the first place, pain can serve as a protection from greater damage. When we inadvertently touch a flame or hot stove we can be grateful for the hurt and the immediate reflex that limits the harm to a blister. We can be grateful for the sprain that results from the twisting of a wrist or the turning of an ankle. The immediate and intense pain keeps us from further harm. The continuing pain forces us to relieve the damaged member so that proper healing can take place. Thus, pain can carry the value of protection.

Suffering may have value also when it forces us to recognize our dependence upon God. Isn't it true that we have a way of running things our own way until all goes wrong? Then we bring God into the act. It sometimes takes suffering to bring us to a sense of dependence. This dependence in turn puts us in an attitude of prayer which has a healing quality about it. Suffering may not be relieved immediately, but its poisoning effects within us are neutralized.

A third value which may grow out of suffering is the sympathetic response of observers. Do you remember the "Hiroshima Maidens"? These were the twenty-five young women who had been terribly disfigured by the blast of the atomic bomb and were subsequently brought to the United States by private citizens. American surgeons then donated their skills to the healing of these unfortunate girls. Plastic surgery made it possible for them to live full lives back in their homeland. Their suffering had been real, and so was their healing. But there was great value to those who gave of their funds and their skills to these women. We have an innate desire to help the unfortunate and the harmed, especially the young and innocent. We are enriched when we wipe the tear of an unfortunate child, give to the needy, and comfort those among us who are distressed.

A fourth value to be gained from suffering is the possibility of new learning. Experience has been noted as the best teacher. Unfortunately, many of the most effective teaching experiences are costly and painful. Ralph Waldo Emerson put it this way: "Bad times have a scientific value. These are occasions a good learner would not miss."

A fifth potential value is that new life can emerge from suffering. Every mother who has suffered the pangs of childbirth understands this. Both individual Christians and church congregations can coast comfortably through time without exemplifying spiritual life and vitality. Sometimes new life and progress are possible only through experiences of pain and pressure.

An unusual evergreen which is common throughout Yellowstone Park is the lodgepole pine. The cones of this tree may remain on the tree for years, and they do not open even when they fall from the tree. They open only as a result of contact with intense heat. A forest fire will at once destroy all the vegetation in its path, and at the same time open the cones of these lodgepole pines. The continuing life of these trees results from an experience of death.

All of this is to say that pain can have some good results. But these results cannot be considered the purpose of pain. So what is the purpose? Why is there misery? What did Jesus say?

What Jesus Didn't Teach

We may well begin by indicating what Jesus did *not* teach about suffering. First, Jesus did not teach that sickness is a punishment. It is a common misconception that suffering is a proof of wrongdoing and a punishment sent by God. The friends of Job tried to convince him that his suffering was the result of his sin. But we cannot read of Jesus' healings and think that those whom he helped were being punished by God. If we did, Jesus' healings would be an undoing of God's righteous punishments!

Jesus denies explicitly that sickness and suffering are the direct results of a person's sin. The early verses of Luke 13 describe his teachings concerning this matter:

> There were some present at that very time who told him of the Galileans whose blood Pilate had mingled with their sacrifices. And he answered them, "Do you think that these Galileans were worse sinners than all the other Galileans, because they suffered thus? I tell you, No; but unless you repent you will all likewise perish" (Luke 13:1–3).

Jesus refutes the idea that God was responsible for the calamities that fell upon the people of Galilee and Jerusalem. They were, rather, the unfortunate victims of a monstrous man and a fatal accident.

In the second place, Jesus did not teach that sickness is a sign of our parents' sin. In John's Gospel we read of a man who was born blind and who was healed by Jesus. The disciples of Jesus assumed that this man's physical limitation was the result of some wrongdoing. Their question was whether this sin was his or his ancestor's. Thus, they asked, "Rabbi, who sinned, this man or his parents, that he was born blind?" (John 9:2). Inasmuch as he was *born* blind, his own sin would have to have been in his prenatal state or even in some previous life.

Jesus was not interested in speculative discussion about this particular question. He answered, "It was not that this man sinned, or his parents, but that the works of God might be made manifest in him. We must work the works of him who sent me, while it is day . . ." (John 9:3–4). And this he did. He healed the man.

Rather than spending time and energy in a theological discussion about the unknown origin of this man's disability, Jesus was concerned with the man's problem and with that of his accusers. The religious leadership had cut Jesus off from their community. They claimed that he was both a sinner and one who refused their authority. Their figurative blindness was reflected in their rejection of Jesus and his work. Jesus confronted them, and they got the message: "Are we also blind?" they asked. Jesus responded, "If you were blind, you would have no guilt; but now that you say, 'We see,' your guilt remains" (John 9:40, 41). The smug and so-called good people of the community are too often afraid of the potential guilt that would be incurred by associating with the wrong people. If these people had recognized that they were needy, they could have been forgiven and helped. However, they were sure that they were both good and without need; thus, there was no help that could be effective for them.

Jesus had another word for those of us who are critical of others.

> "Why do you see the speck that is in your brother's eye, but do not notice the log that is in your own eye? Or how can you say to your brother, 'Let me take the speck out of your eye,' when there is a log in your own eye? You hypocrite, first take the log out of your own eye, and then you will see clearly to take the speck out of your brother's eye" (Matthew 7:3–5).

Jesus uses a humorous caricature in order for us to see ourselves as being unfairly critical. Even ostensibly good people can be spiritually blind—"blind leaders of the blind" he called them (Matthew 15:14; Luke 6:39). It is not our task to seek out the source of a person's sickness. Rather, we are to see our own wrongs before God and seek divine healing and strength.

In the third place, Jesus did not teach that God causes all sickness. God has created a world in which sickness, suffering, and wrongdoing can exist; but God is not directly responsible for such things. Jesus taught that God is the conqueror, not the cause, of sickness. In the story of the healing of the man born blind, Jesus spoke of this healing as working "the works of him who sent me, while it is day; night comes, when no one can work. As long as I am in the world, I am the light of the world" (John 9:4–5).

We note, in the fourth place, that Jesus did not give us a philosophy about suffering. We might expect the master teacher to clothe human suffering with a sense of meaning. Rather than giving meaning to the problem of suffering, he gives *us* meaning by relating himself personally with us. This relationship is reflected in one of his most familiar statements.

"Come unto me, all ye that labor and are heavy laden, and I will give you rest. Take my yoke upon you, and learn of me; for I am meek and lowly in heart: and ye shall find rest unto your souls. For my yoke is easy, and my burden is light" (Matthew 11:28–30).

Archbishop Romero was a man who stood in the midst of and on behalf of his people in the name of his Lord. He was shot to death by gunmen while saying mass in his cathedral. Jesus made no attempt to explain theologically or philosophically this kind of death. But he gave himself for and related himself with those who would follow him in such witness. The occasion of Romero's death brought forth the following words from the pen of Edith Lovejoy Pierce:

> Why must the good men die before their time,
> While evil men, the cancerous souls
> In rotting bodies, linger on
> To poison and infect the world?
> Why?
> *Why* is a meaningless word,
> Its meaning blotted out by blood on stones.
> Step by step, the argument
> Rises in a bitter steep ascent
> To the bare hill
> Whereon the mind, blown wide,
> Touches the cross
> On which the Best Man died.[1]

Jesus was tested in all points as we are. He suffered and died as a man. Remember the anguished cry of the bereaved parent, "Where was God when my son was killed?" The answer is not a philosophical one or even a completely satisfying one at the intellectual level. It is the answer of experience. God was in the same place when God's only Son was killed.

So Jesus did not teach that the source of suffering is in our wrongdoing or in that of our parents. He did not teach that God causes all sickness, and he did not teach a philosophy about suffering in order that we might understand the rationale involved in the evils of our world. What then did he teach about suffering?

Jesus taught—and showed—us how to *react* to suffering. Any good which comes from suffering is not because suffering itself is good, but because we react positively and constructively within suffering. It is this response that is good, not the suffering itself.

Dr. Elisabeth Kubler–Ross has attained international recognition through her work in understanding the process of dying and her concern for relieving the mental suffering of the terminally ill. Her work, *On Death and Dying,* was the result of an interdisciplinary seminar on death at the University of Chicago.[2] Dr. Ross is fond of pointing out that we are like stained glass windows. We reflect some light when the sun is out, but when darkness comes our true beauty is seen only if there is light within.

W. Somerset Maugham presents a negative view of human suffering in the concluding chapter of his *The Moon and Sixpence.* "It is not true that suffering ennobles the character; happiness does that sometimes, but suffering, for the most part, makes men petty and vindictive."[3]

Our responses to suffering are many. The most common is that of self–pity. "Why did God ever allow this to happen to me?" You have heard it before, perhaps you have even said it; and certainly you have felt it. But there is nothing constructive about this attitude.

Some respond to suffering by denying that it is real. But this is also an inadequate response to the problem. Even if evil is all in our minds, the evil that is in your mind is still great enough to create all types of havoc. The harm done by this evil is just as great as any harm done by objective wrongdoing. Then, of course, we must remember that if evil is only an error in our thinking, this error had to come from some place. Where could it come from in a world that is perfect—in which there is no evil? No, it is unrealistic, unbiblical, and unlike the reaction of Jesus to deny the reality of evil.

Others of us respond to suffering by trying to escape it. We try to take the anesthetic route. Some Christians expect God to deliver them from all suffering. But the servant is not above the master. Jesus' ministry, particularly the road toward his death, was one of suffering. There is no guarantee that Christians in the twentieth century will be delivered from the burdens borne by the martyrs and the faithful. The Christian response to suffering is not one of determined divine deliverance.

The opposite of the response of escape would be the response of endurance. Thus, there are some who believe that Jesus teaches us to endure pain either stoically or piously. "Keep a stiff upper lip. Chin up, chest out. Come what may, I can take anything!" You have heard it before. Many of us say it, but we don't really mean it, not down deep.

Then there is pious endurance. Whatever the problem the response is, "It was the will of God." Sounds devoted, doesn't it? A child is run down by a careless driver. The response of some pious bystander, "It was the will of God." The words are almost blasphemous. They assume that God wills all of the suffering in the world. They assume that the world moves on in a fatalistic pattern with every detail determined in advance by God. The pious response assumes that there is no demonic element, no wrong in the world, that everything—good and evil—is determined by God. Not so the teaching of Jesus. On the contrary, Jesus healed. Disease was a trespasser which had no rights within the reign of God. Indeed, part of the Good News which Jesus came to proclaim was that of healing.

The Role of Suffering

Now if Jesus did not teach these responses to suffering, what did he teach? How should we respond to suffering? His teaching—and indeed, his very being—reflected a sublimation of suffering. We are to turn evil into good. Suffering is not to be escaped or endured, but to be transformed. It is to be used.

Meaningful suffering is reflected in the Old Testament in the person of Joseph. His brothers had sold him as a slave. God intervened, however, and Joseph had been freed in Egypt. Ultimately, he was elevated until he was second only to the king. In the course of time his brothers faced him, and he made himself known to them. In the final chapter of the book of Genesis we read that his brothers came and fell down before him. Evidently, they feared for their lives. Joseph responded by indicating that they should not fear. His interpretation of the entire matter is described in Genesis 50:20. "As for you, you meant evil against me; but God meant it for good. . . ." This statement also reflects Jesus' life. It sums up his attitude toward suffering in all of his teachings.

Nor is this idea about the role of suffering only the teaching of Scripture. It is confirmed by modern therapists and sensitive observers of human nature. Note two such witnesses. First, Rollo May:

> People then should rejoice in suffering, strange as it sounds, for this is a sign of the availability of energy to transform their characters. Suffering is nature's way of indicating a mistaken attitude or way of behavior, and . . . to the non–egocentric person every moment of suffering is the opportunity for growth.[4]

Second, Dorothy Berkely Phillips:

> This drastic experience we call the major crisis. All egocentricity leads toward it. Moreover, it should be welcomed; for through its suffering, as will be seen, we may move into that joy and peace which comes from releasing the self within from the limitations of its shell into the creative, productive, courageous, loving expressions of which it is capable. That is indeed the abundant life.[5]

If we are to use suffering for good, we must make certain assumptions about God's ways of working. We must assume, in the first place, that God knows all. This was the point of Jesus' teachings that God knows about every sparrow that falls to the ground (Matthew 10:29; Luke 12:6).

God does not protect all birds from harm. Rather, God is concerned and knows about the harm that comes upon all creatures. This is what we must believe.

Second, we should assume that God has all power. We should believe that God both cares and will care. In the strength of the Almighty, and under divine guidance, we can use evil for good. This belief in God's power does not demand God's intimate control of all details. That is, every problem is not solved by God. Our

Creator has given us freedom. But God does have the last word. God can and does transform "wrongs."

Jesus' teaching concerning the role of suffering is perhaps most clear in his description of the faithful witness of his followers. Here is what he told them:

> "But before all this they will lay their hands on you and persecute you, delivering you up to the synagogues and prisons, and you will be brought before kings and governors for my name's sake. This will be a time for you to bear testimony" (Luke 21:12–13).

If I had said this, it would not have occurred to me to include this last sentence. But Jesus did. In short, he indicates that when all the problems and perplexities of life are upon us, when suffering and sin have taken their toll, then we are to use this as a time for witness. The calamities and catastrophies are to be used for good.

Edwin Markham presents this point in verse:

> Defeat may serve as well as victory
> To shake the soul and let the glory out.
> When the great oak is straining in the wind,
> The boughs drink in new beauty, and the trunk
> Sends down a deeper root on the windward side.
> Only the soul that knows the mighty grief
> Can know the mighty rapture. Sorrows come
> To stretch out spaces in the heart for joy.[6]

The ancestors and relatives of the modern Baptist movement reflected such suffering in witness. Cardinal Hosius, the pope's representative at the Council of Trent, explained the growth of these believers in the following words:

> If the truth of religion were to be judged by the readiness and boldness which a man of any sect shows in suffering, then the opinion and persuasion of no sect can be truer and surer than that of the Anabaptists since there have been none for these twelve hundred years past, that have been more generally punished or that have more cheerfully and steadfastly undergone and even offered themselves to the most cruel sorts of punishment than these people.[7]

Felix Manta, for example, was sentenced the year preceding the Council to be drowned for the crime of believer's baptism. Led through the streets of Zurich, he preached to the people as he went.

His elderly mother and brother, brushing away their tears, walked by his side exhorting him to suffer bravely for Jesus' sake.

Twentieth–century Methodist historian Frank S. Mead describes the Baptist movement in these words:

> The world has done its best to stop them; we can trace their history more readily in the bloody footprints of their martyrs than in the ink of their historians. We have tried to shame them by whipping them and they have made us ashamed of our whipping–posts. We chained them in jail and discovered that the other end of the chain was fast about our own necks. We let their blood in Boston and the South, only to find the fairest American flowers we know growing from that very soil. Addlepated world! You tried to stamp them out and all you got for it was to have them leave their stamp on you![8]

Jesus exercised his ministry in a context of pressure and was often under attack. You will remember that he told three beautiful stories about the lost which are found in Luke 15. These three included the story of the one lost sheep that had gone astray, but which was found by the shepherd and returned. Then there was the story of the coin that the woman sought until she found it and rejoiced. Finally, there is what has been called the most beautiful story in the world, the story about the wayward, or prodigal, son. All three of these stories grow out of a circumstance that was intended to embarrass Jesus. The account begins: "Now the tax collectors and sinners were all drawing near to hear him. And the Pharisees and the scribes murmured, saying, 'This man receives sinners and eats with them.' So he told them this parable . . ." (Luke 15:1–3). These beautiful stories, which have been used for the blessing of the world, grew out of a circumstance that was supposed to bring embarrassment and pain to Jesus.

Tension, pressure, and suffering are paramount in both Jesus' teaching and life. Is this not the essence of the cross? Those who put him there meant it for evil, but God turned it to good.

Jesus' entire public ministry was an anticipation of the cross. The early portion of Jesus' ministry was geared to helping the multitudes and leading his disciples to understand who he was.

Their understanding climaxed with the statement of Peter, "You are the Christ, the Son of the living God" (Matthew 16:16). This confession became both a high point and a transition point in Jesus' ministry.

The more surprising thing is the teaching that immediately followed this confession.

> From that time Jesus began to show his disciples that he must go to Jerusalem and suffer many things from the elders and chief priests and scribes, and be killed, and on the third day be raised (Matthew 16:21; Mark 8:31; Luke 9:22).

Again, in all three of these accounts we read that Jesus went immediately to the Mount of Transfiguration. Here he was shown in the most glorious state in which his disciples ever observed him. He was speaking in this exalted situation with Moses and Elijah, the notable Old Testament leaders. And what were they talking about?—His death! Out of this discussion of the greatest agony imaginable comes the greatest ecstasy and transfiguration possible. A conversation concerning an evil was being used for good.

Such changing of evil to good was ultimately exemplified in the cross. Here the Gospels make it clear that God acted in a unique manner for the redemption of the world. Jesus took the place of suffering and used it as a lever by which he moved the entire world toward God. The cross was an ugly death. There was no good to be seen or felt in this agony and ignominy. But God made it glorious. The greatest of human evils God turned to the greatest good. This is the Good News! Our sins and the suffering of God's only begotten have been turned into our salvation.

So it was in Jesus—the one who was the best—that we see the greatest amount of suffering. When all the powers of evil did their worst, God was doing the greatest work for us. When Jesus felt most forsaken, God was most near, effecting your redemption and mine.

Chapter Eight

Does God Answer Prayer?

The Teachings of Jesus Concerning Prayer

———⚜———

W ho prays? Far fewer of us than we might imagine. Ministers of the gospel pray less than they would like.
My first meeting with Ruell Howe was in a small retreat of ministers. Howe challenged us with the statement, "Ministers don't pray!" He went on to explain his statement by saying that ministers likely spent more time in public prayer than in personal devotion.

Moreover, ministers often miss those opportunities of meaningful prayer with and in behalf of others. Gene Bartlett's recounting of this experience only serves to demonstrate our common failure:

Every week for several years I called on a member of our congregation who was in a nursing home. To reach her room, I passed the open door of another room and often noticed a woman in a wheelchair seated by the window. When I stopped one day to greet her, I saw that paralysis had robbed her of her ability to speak. Yet each time I stopped at her door, spoke to her, then went on to make my call. One day after I had greeted her in this way, something caught my attention on my way out. When I stopped at the door for the second time, by inarticulate sound and movement of her chair, it was evident that she wanted me to come in. When I stood beside her chair, she nodded to the pencil tablet on her lap. I picked it up to discover that she had managed to scrawl a single word in large letters:

'Prayer.' It brought back poignant memories of all the times I had stopped by her doorway and engaged in some passing small talk! All the time she had waited and hoped for 'more' which prayer assumes. [1]

The Christian laity fares no better. We don't pray, at least, not as often as our forebears did. Is our lack of prayer because we are "grown," more mature? We don't feel the need that our grandparents did. We understand—and even control—elements of the universe that seemed mysterious to them.

We have become an extremely naturalistic and materialistic people. Since we control so much of our environment, we may legitimately ask if it is necessary—or even proper—to ask for help. Should we pray for things? Jesus says we should pray, even for "daily bread." Can we include our circumstances in our prayers? Jesus said "whatever you ask" (Mark 11:24) is appropriate. We may legitimately expect some spiritual and psychological benefits as the results of our praying. Serenity and calm, vision and enthusiasm, strength and courage—these we can expect from the time of prayer. But can we ask for more?

A Life of Prayer

We can hardly do better than to review Jesus' teachings and actions concerning prayer. His works and words are closely related here, as they are elsewhere in his ministry. The writers of the Gospels enable us to observe Jesus at prayer. They also share with us much of the teaching concerning prayer that he presented to his disciples.

There numerous occasions when Jesus prayed. Before we consider his teachings about prayer, we can learn much by observing him within his own experience of prayer.

When Jesus Prayed

The first thing we should notice is that Jesus prayed regularly. You may remember reading about one exceptional day in the ministry of Jesus as recorded in the last half of the first chapter of Mark. It had been an extremely busy Sabbath day. At last, it was the evening, and Mark tells us that the "whole city was gathered together about the door. And he healed many who were sick with various diseases" (Mark 1:33–34). We might expect that he would sleep late the next morning. On the contrary, we read that "in the morning, a great while before day, he rose and went out to a lonely place, and there he prayed" (Mark 1:35).

This moving from multitude to solitude is a mark of Jesus' ministry. Fellowship with God was basic. Nor was this true only of the beginning of his ministry. Throughout Jesus' life we see this movement from the pressure of need to the presence of God. The sense of tiredness, the need of rest, the pressure of tasks undone—these could not keep him from that better part; rather, they drove him to the place of prayer.

Our need is even greater, as is our sense of distance from God. The essence of prayer is the closing of this gap, the practicing of the presence of God.

There is a well-known prayer used by French seafarers: "O God, thy sea is so great and my boat is so small!" That's the entire prayer. Some would say it is too short to be a prayer. But this is the essence of practicing God's presence—recognizing our inadequacy in the presence of God.

This sense of presence should also be marked with persistence. Not all prayers are formal. Victor Hugo put it well: "Certain thoughts are prayers. There are moments when, whatever be the attitude of the body, the soul is on its knees."

There was a high correlation between Jesus' prayer life and public ministry. His action grew out of prayer, and his prayers drove him to action. Dr. G. Campbell Morgan liked to tell of the young girl whose brother had set a trap to ensnare birds in their garden. She berated his cruelty and let it be known that she was praying that he would catch no birds. Finally, she announced that her prayer had been answered. "How do you know that no birds will be caught?" her parents asked. "Because," she answered triumphantly, "last night I went out and smashed the trap!"

J. Hudson Taylor made the point with greater theological sophistication. "It is possible to work without prayer," he said. "It is a bad plan, but it can be done. But you cannot pray without working."

At this point we should note that prayer and ministry are related, but not identical. Jesus took time to pray. He did not substitute activity for prayer. He sensed that our bodies are the living sacrifice of which Paul wrote. He saw service as an offering presented in the presence of God, but refused the snare of what Evelyn Underwood has called the "forsaking of the Lord in order to enter his service." He rolled up his sleeves, but he also bent his knees.

Beyond his regular practice of prayer, Jesus gave himself to prayer upon special occasions. This was particularly true in times of difficulty and decision. The primary points of decision in Jesus' ministry included his initial ministry in Capernaum, the selection of the twelve disciples, Peter's confession of him as the Christ, his transfiguration, and his approaching agony on the cross. It is striking that Jesus anticipation or contemplation of each of these events was marked by his withdrawal in order that he might give himself to prayer. We shall briefly note each of these key events.

Jesus' public ministry was begun when he presented himself to John for baptism in the Jordan River. When Luke describes Jesus' baptism, he adds that he was praying when "the heaven was opened, and the Holy Spirit descended" (Luke 3:21–22). This descent of the Spirit reflects a significant spiritual experience as Jesus' vocation was announced. This determining of life's work—one of the most important decisions that each of us must make—was for Jesus a time of prayer and revelation.

We have already noted that busy first day in Capernaum; Jesus retired from the multitudes in order that he might involve himself in prayer. The problem is obvious. Mark tells us that "he healed many who were sick with various diseases" (Mark 1:34). We may be sure that the pressure for continued healings would be great. Jesus was forced to consider the relative values of his healing ministry and of his teaching activity. The multitudes would make it impossible for him to enter into the ministry of teaching concerning the kingdom of God. The decision could only be made apart from the crowds and in the presence of his God. When his followers found him in the place of prayer, he said, "Let us go on to the next towns, that I may preach there also; for that is why I came out" (Mark 1:38). So the direction and emphasis of Jesus' ministry were determined in prayer.

The next significant time of decision was the determination of the personnel to be included in his band of disciples. That the selection of his disciples was also rooted in prayer is made clear by Luke: "In these days he went out to the mountain to pray; and all night he continued in prayer to God. And when it was day, he called his disciples, and chose from them twelve, whom he named apostles" (Luke 6:12, 13).

The outstanding transitional point in Jesus' ministry is commonly called the Great Confession. He had taught and served the multitudes in the presence of his disciples over the months and even years. Finally, he asked his followers who they thought he was. Peter, responding for the group, indicated that Jesus was the Christ who was sent from God. This was a climactic point in Jesus' ministry. It is clear that Jesus' presentation of the question to the disciples was rooted in a special time of prayer. Luke tells us that

> . . . as he was praying alone the disciples were with him; and he asked them, "Who do the people say that I am?" And they answered, "John the Baptist; but others say, Elijah; and others, that one of the old prophets has risen." And he said to them, "But who do you say that I am?" And Peter answered, "The Christ of God" (Luke 9:18–20).

Certainly one of the most spectacular events in the career of Jesus was his transfiguration on a mountain. If we are to follow Luke's explanation, the purpose of the ascent of the mountain was to pray. Luke tells us that "he took with him Peter and John and James, and went up on the mountain to pray. And as he was praying, the appearance of his countenance was altered, and his raiment became dazzling white" (Luke 9:28–29). On this occasion of his glory, he spoke with Moses and Elijah. They "spoke of his departure, which he was to accomplish at Jerusalem" (Luke 9:31). The glory of the transfiguration was the outgrowth of a retreat for the purpose of prayer. At the same time we note that the conversation involved in Jesus' transfiguration concerned his coming death. It was this decision—to face Jerusalem and its fatal consequences—that both necessitated a time of prayer and was forged in prayer.

The decision to move to Calvary was strengthened and consummated in the Garden of Gethsemane. The pressure of the hour and the agony of the expectation are obvious as Jesus anticipated the cross. His prayer of decision is familiar: "Father, if thou art willing, remove this cup from me; nevertheless not my will, but thine, be done" (Luke 22:42). Thus, the time of Jesus' most agonizing decision was marked by prayer.

Prayer was also central at the cross, as we might expect. We are familiar with the so-called seven last words from the cross. They are the statements that fell from the lips of Jesus while he was suspended and undergoing the pain of death. These statements are actually a series of prayers. Forsaken by others, he continued relating with God. Even his cry of dereliction, "My God, my God, why hast thou forsaken me?" (Matthew 27:46), was a prayer.

How Jesus Prayed

Thus far we have noted *when* Jesus prayed. Prayer was a regular experience for him. In addition, he gave himself more significantly to prayer at the decision points within his ministry. We can now turn our attention to *how* Jesus prayed. The two most obvious, and perhaps unexpected, elements in Jesus' prayers are their brevity and their spontaneity. Jesus' prayers, as recorded in the Gospels, are extremely short.

The best known of these prayers, of course, is that which we call the Lord's Prayer. This is not so much a prayer that Jesus prayed as one he presented to his disciples as a pattern for their prayers. To us, this is an extremely brief prayer. It can normally be said in less than twenty seconds. But the striking thing is this: The Lord's Prayer is the longest of Jesus' recorded prayers! Many of them are only one sentence. The only exception is recorded in John 17 when Jesus prayed with and for his disciples on his last night with them. Even so, this exception seems to demonstrate the rule. Jesus prayed briefly.

His rationale for brevity in prayer was expressed in his Sermon on the Mount. He exhorted.

> "And in praying do not heap up empty phrases as the Gentiles do; for they think that they will be heard for their many words. Do not be like them, for your Father knows what you need before you ask Him" (Matthew 6:7, 8).

This exhortation seems to reflect Jesus' own reason for direct-ness in prayer. He was in close fellowship with God. The closest relationships are often cemented in silence and only confused with excessive talk. Jesus' prayers were not given to argumentation with God or to the smoke screen of many words. They were, clearly, not public demonstrations.

Old hands in Washington like to tell of the time when Bill Moyers was a special assistant to President Lyndon B. Johnson. Since Moyers had received theological training and had served as a Bap-tist minister in Texas, he was asked to say grace before a meal in the family quarters of the White House. When Moyers prayed softly, the President interrupted with, "Speak up, Bill! Speak up!" Moy-ers refrained from looking up and stopped his prayer only long enough to say, "I wasn't addressing you, Mr. President."

Jesus' praying was as informal and direct as it was brief. A mod-ern prayer book would hardly include the prayers of Jesus—except, of course, the Lord's Prayer and the so–called "high priestly prayer" of John 17. The informality of his prayers suggests the concerns of the moment and the constancy of his sense of relation-ship with God.

What Jesus Prayed About

At this point we may well turn our attention to the contents of Jesus' prayers. For what did he pray? There were at least four ele-ments in his prayers. First and basic was the element of thanksgiv-ing. "I thank thee, Father, Lord of heaven and earth, that thou hast hidden these things from the wise and understanding and revealed them to babes; yea, Father, for such was thy gracious will" (Luke 10:21). Similarly the last night in the upper room found him giving thanks for the bread and the cup.

Second, the prayers of Jesus reflected communion and commit-ment. We have already noticed that he prayed on the Mount of Transfiguration. Some have suggested that such praying and com-munion were normal with Jesus, and that his transfiguration was something of an afterglow which resulted from this communion. (The Gospels see more in this event. The transfiguration also reflected Jesus' messianic office and approaching death.) Indeed,

Jesus sensed his fellowship with God even in the shadow of the cross. There, his final words were those of commitment: "Father, into thy hands I commit my spirit!" (Luke 23:46).

Third, and most commonly, Jesus' prayers included intercession. He prayed mainly for others. He even included those who were responsible for his being on the cross in his prayer: "Father, forgive them; for they know not what they do" (Luke 23:34). We have already noted that he prayed for his disciples, and in particular, he prayed for Peter who was to deny him.

> "Simon, Simon, behold, Satan demanded to have you, that he might sift you like wheat, but I have prayed for you that your faith may not fail; and when you have turned again, strengthen your brethren" (Luke 22:31, 32).

And who can forget that Jesus prayed for little children, taking them up in his arms and blessing them?

Finally, we should notice that Jesus' prayers related to his own needs. This was most clear in the Garden of Gethsemane when he cried: "My Father, if it be possible, let this cup pass from me; nevertheless, not as I will, but as thou wilt" (Matthew 26:39).

Thus far we have noted when, how, and for what Jesus prayed. He prayed both regularly and in times of great decision. His prayers were short and spontaneous. He prayed in a spirit of thanksgiving and fellowship with God, and he prayed both for others and for his own needs. We now turn our attention to his teachings concerning prayer.

Why Jesus Prayed

Jesus' teachings about prayer grew out of his experience of prayer. Luke describes this event: "He was praying in a certain place, and when he ceased, one of his disciples said to him, 'Lord, teach us to pray, as John taught his disciples.'" (Luke 11:1). The response to their request was the presentation of the Lord's Prayer (Luke 11:2–4; Matthew 6:9–13). This does not mean, of course, that the disciples had not prayed up to this time. On the contrary, there were certain ritualistic prayers of the Jewish people that had been common to them since childhood. There is even the probability that the disciples, devoted to the purposes of God as they were, involved themselves in a personal discipline of prayer. They recognized, however, that there was a clear distinction between their method and attitude in prayer and that of Jesus. This obvious difference brought forth their request. They wanted to pray as he did. If we share this desire, we can hardly do better than to pattern our prayer experience after that of the Lord's Prayer.

There are two basic elements in the Lord's Prayer, as there should be in our own. Three statements are given to each of these elements. First, the prayer recognizes the greatness of God. Second, the prayer reflects human need. The order is important. Before we ask for personal needs, Jesus taught, we should root ourselves and our concerns in the purposes of God.

The first three petitions reflect the greatness of God and relate to the divine name, kingdom, and will. Indeed, these petitions, presumptuous as it may seem, are prayer in behalf of God. Dr. Maxie Gordon has given years to preparing black leaders at Benedict College. He tells of the girl who rose from her prayers only to return to her knees to add a P.S.: "By the way, God, take care of yourself, because if anything happens to you, we are all in a mess." This observation is underscored in the first half of the Lord's Prayer.

First, "Hallowed be thy name." The concern is that God's name be recognized as holy throughout the world. It is a request that all people everywhere will acknowledge God's sovereignty. The "name" in Jewish society was far more important than we consider it today. The name reflected the character, the person. This statement is a request that we recognize the holiness of God and relate to the Holy One accordingly.

Second, "Thy kingdom come." Many expected this to be a political kingdom in which God would show divine power through a chosen people. Jesus makes it clear that this kingdom is rooted in the hearts and the wills of those who respond to God in faith and personal commitment. The prayer is that this kingdom will come through the lives of the faithful.

Third, "Thy will be done." God's will must first be done in our own experience. Then we should pray that it would be so in the experience of all persons and in every area of life. It is prayer in this dimension that marks the great moments of the church. John

Erskine, an Edinburgh minister of the early eighteenth century, published a plea to the people of Scotland to unite in prayer. When Jonathan Edwards read this plea, he wrote a response entitled, *A Humble Attempt to Promote Explicit Agreement and Visible Union of All God's People in Extraordinary Prayer for the Revival of Religion and the Advancement of Christ's Kingdom on Earth, pursuant to Scripture Promises and Prophecies Concerning the Last Time.* The attempt, though verbose for modern taste, nevertheless eventuated in the Great Awakening.

It is only when our concerns are truly rooted in the nature, purposes, and will of God that we can ask appropriately for our personal desires and needs. Once we have rooted our experience in the purposes of God, we can anticipate providential care.

The three personal petitions are also well known. First, "Give us this day our daily bread." If our concerns are rooted in God's purposes, we have a right to ask for our personal, daily needs. Second, "Forgive us our debts, As we also have forgiven our debtors." We need forgiveness, and we must also be forgiving. Indeed, if we fail to recognize our relationship with others and are unwilling to forgive them, we can hardly appreciate our relationship with the forgiving Lord and sense our own forgiveness (Matthew 6:14–15). Third, "Lead us not into temptation, But deliver us from evil." Just as the second request is for forgiveness for past sins, this third request is for deliverance from future sins. Our English word "lead" gives the impression that God may guide us into sin. The Aramaic language which Jesus spoke, however, does not give this impression. It does not assume that God is the cause of our temptation. The meaning is more like: "Don't let us come into temptation."

This most familiar prayer is introduced with a recognition of God as Father, and continues with three statements of concern with reference to God's character, kingdom, and will. The prayer then itemizes three requests for personal needs of subsistence, forgiveness, and guidance, and concludes with a statement of praise and glory to God. (This concluding statement is not found in the Lord's Prayer as recorded in Luke's Gospel. Indeed, it is not found in many of the earliest Greek manuscripts of Matthew's Gospel. It is probable that this conclusion was added very early when the Lord's Prayer was changed from a personal prayer to a group prayer. It was used liturgically by groups of Christians in worship, much as we use this prayer in our church services today. Thus, this final addition, though probably not given by Jesus in his original statement of the Lord's Prayer, still fits the essential spirit and purpose of this prayer.)

Much more can be said about Jesus' teachings concerning prayer. His teachings emphasize prayer as part of a personal relationship with God. Second, they emphasize an attitude of humility in prayer. Third, they represent the attitude of prayer as love toward our sisters and brothers in the faith. The final attitude—and perhaps the most surprising emphasis of Jesus—is that of persistence. Jesus indicates quite clearly that we should continue to pray and stay in the presence of God (Luke 11:5-13; 18:1-8). Indeed, the sense of the presence of God is the essence of prayer.

We have reviewed both Jesus' activities and his teachings concerning prayer. If we pattern our experience after Jesus' activities and teachings, we shall find that all of life becomes a prayer—a sense of the presence of God. Moreover, we shall know the truth observed by Alfred Lord Tennyson in his description of the passing of Arthur:

> More things are wrought by prayer
> Than this world dreams of.
> Wherefore, let thy voice
> Rise like a fountain for me night and day.
> For what are men better than sheep or goats
> That nourish a blind life within the brain,
> If, knowing God, they lift not hands of prayer
> Both for themselves and those who call them friend?[2]

Chapter Nine

What About the Old Testament?

The Teachings of Jesus Concerning the Old Testament

W hat is the value and authority of the Old Testament for Christians? We might ask the question because of the assumption that "new" is better than "old." Some would go so far as to say that the New Testament is the Christian Bible, while the Old Testament is the Jewish Bible which also carries authority for our Moslem friends. We infer or assume that the New Testament is superior to the Old Testament simply because it is new.

On the other hand, we speak about the old–time religion with a sense of nostalgia. In this instance we feel that the old carries elements of superiority over the new. But how old do we want our old–time religion to be? Do we want that of our parents or of our great-grandparents? We should be satisfied with neither. The old–time religion, if it is to be properly understood, must be a good bit older—two thousand years older! If we want an old–time religion that is really vital we must go beyond the accretions of our traditions to a time long ago and a place far away. We must see Jesus walking dusty roads with a dozen followers; and we must understand that the Eternal was, in Jesus, nearer than ever among the people of God. But once we go back to a religion that old, we find that it is even older. Jesus was constantly rooting his teachings in and guiding his ministry by the spiritual experience of an earlier time. His insights and activities were deeply rooted in what we call the Old Testament.

The term "Old Testament" comes from a statement of the apostle Paul in his second letter to the Corinthian Christians. He was concerned about his Jewish friends who failed to see that Jesus Christ was the One who was anticipated in the Hebrew Bible (the Old Testament). In expressing his concern for his compatriots he indicated that their minds were veiled "when they read the old covenant" (2 Corinthians 3:14). So he referred to the Bible that was given to the Jewish people as "the old covenant" or "the Old Testament." The words "covenant" and "testament" are interchangeable in the Bible. Biblically speaking, a covenant is different from a legal contract. A contract determines or limits legal claims that two parties may have toward one another. A covenant relates people to one another or even to God in positive and voluntary ways. A contract exerts control. A covenant relates us to one another as human beings in trust and faithfulness. Roth and Ruether explain:

> In our time, church manuals sometimes refer to the marriage union as a covenant between a man and woman. . . . It is not a vaguely defined relationship which can be ignored in unfavorable circumstances or canceled at will. A covenant is a communion between partners, solemnly initiated, binding the partners into a new pattern of life, and letting them mutually define each other. It affects all aspects of the partners' lives, creating between and for them a sphere of interaction in loyalty to each other.[1]

Paul's reference to the Hebrew Bible as the "old covenant" carried with it an adhesive quality. The term stuck! We commonly refer to the Hebrew Bible and its translations as the "Old Testament."

Jeremiah, who began his prophetic ministry during the reign and religious revival of Josiah, spoke of the days to come when God would "make a new covenant with the house of Israel and the house of Judah" (Jeremiah 31:31). In his last night with the disciples Jesus affirmed that this promised new covenant was being fulfilled in himself. Thus, when he anticipated the Communion service at the Last Supper, he spoke of the wine as "the new covenant in my blood" (1 Corinthians 11:25). Jesus, himself, is the new covenant of the New Testament. Inasmuch as the writings of his immediate followers reflect his life and teachings so closely we now refer to them as the "New Testament." All of this is to say that the terms "Old Testament" and "New Testament," as originally given to us by Paul and Jesus, are not set against one another. On the contrary, the Old Testament and the New Testament are essentially related. It has been well said that "the New Testament is in the Old contained, and the Old Testament is in the New explained."

Jesus quoted and interpreted the Old Testament with great reverence. Two things stand out as primary in Jesus' relationship to the Old Testament.

First, he recognized the authority of the Old Testament as sacred Scripture. Josh Billings contended for the authority of Scripture in his "down home" manner: "Allmost enny phool kan prove that the bible ain't true; it takes a wize man to beleave it." The same conviction was expressed in a more sophisticated manner by Adolph Schlatter, the renowned New Testament scholar. He was approached by an admirer who said that he always wanted to meet a theologian who stood upon the Word of God. Schlatter replied, "Thank you. But I don't stand on the Word of God; I stand *under* it."

Second, Jesus anticipated and exemplified the fulfillment of the Old Testament. In Jesus "the Word became flesh" (John 1:14) and thereby fulfilled the Word of God as written in the Old Testament. The entire Bible is the Word of God spoken through the Spirit. Consider the analogy of a short–wave radio. As the operator moves the pointer slowly across the short–wave band dial, there is a soft whisper like a rushing stream. The words are intentionally scrambled for privacy until they are sorted out by the appropriate receiving instrument in the hands of the right person. The speaker at one end of the conversation may be compared to the vital Word of God; the writers are like the sending instrument, giving mixed sounds. The Holy Spirit could be the power that carries the message, and the Bible the receiving instrument in the hands of a person guided by the Holy Spirit. Those outside the fellowship of faith are listeners who hear only the scrambled sounds (1 Corinthians 2:14).

Jesus—Old Testament Scholar

Jesus knew the Hebrew Bible well. He assumed its truth and affirmed its authority. He quoted it and alluded to it regularly, almost unconsciously, throughout his ministry.

It is no easy thing to memorize long passages of Scripture. I remember my shock upon meeting the first person I knew who could quote the entire Old Testament in Hebrew. It was in an advanced Hebrew colloquium. There were several Jewish rabbis and Christian ministers in the course. On occasion the professor was asked for a biblical illustration of the particular grammatical or syntactical point that he was making. Sometimes he was able to illustrate immediately. When he could not, he would turn to a particular student in the class and ask for an illustration. This student would close his eyes and quote the various passages throughout the Old Testament that illustrated the item we were discussing. Soon it became obvious that this man had memorized the entire Hebrew Bible. Moreover, he had become so familiar with it that he could pick out any particular grammatical element and identify the verses containing it. I asked a rabbi who was sitting next to me if this was common. He said that he had some children in his own synagogue school who were able to quote extended sections of the Hebrew Bible.

Jesus used the Scriptures so regularly that we can readily observe his thorough knowledge of them. He may have memorized the Hebrew Bible. In any event, he was completely familiar with the Scriptures. For example, Luke indicates that Jesus entered the synagogue in his home town; "and there was given to him the book of the prophet Isaiah. He opened the book and found the place where it was written . . ." (Luke 4:17). This was far more difficult than it appears. The "book" was in a scroll form. There were no divisions into chapters, and no record of verses. Indeed, there were no separations between the Hebrew words, inasmuch as it was imperative that writers save expensive space. Even so, Jesus was so familiar with the text that he could open the scroll to an exact point the equivalent of sixty pages into the text.

It is also important to remember that obtaining copies of the Scriptures was far more difficult than it is today. We can purchase Bibles at cost from nonprofit organizations such as the American Bible Society. Bibles are available at a smaller cost per page than any other book. But this was not true in the time of Jesus. Every Bible had to be copied by hand. This made them both rare and valuable. They were normally available only in the synagogue.

Jesus' learning of the Old Testament would have been in the synagogue school at Nazareth and in the synagogue services where the Scriptures were read and expounded. It was difficult for a Jewish child to learn the Scriptures outside a classroom. Most of the Bible was learned as it was quoted to the children by the teacher. Jesus must have been a good student. In the Gospels, we find that he quotes from over half of the books of the Old Testament. It is likely that he quoted from more than these. Indeed, our fourth Gospel concludes with the pardonable hyperbole that if the full record of Jesus were "to be written, I suppose that the world itself could not contain the books that would be written" (John 21:25b).

Jesus—Fulfiller of Old Testament Prophecy

Jesus not only knew the Scriptures well, but he saw himself in these Scriptures. His entire ministry—his activities as well as his teachings—grew out of his understanding of the Old Testament.

In the latter portion of the book of Isaiah we read about the "Suffering Servant." Jesus' life and teachings reflected his understanding of the Servant who was to suffer.

We can illustrate Jesus' view of himself as rooted in other Old Testament passages from two specific occasions in his ministry. First, recall the occasion of the imprisonment of John the Baptist. John had served as the primary forerunner of Jesus. He told his followers to look toward Jesus as the One who had come from God. Now, however, John was imprisoned and obviously disheartened. Had he been wrong? Was it possible that Jesus was not the One to come? We read in the Gospel according to Matthew that John "sent word by his disciples and said to him [Jesus], 'Are you he who is to come, or shall we look for another?'" (Matthew 11:2, 3). Jesus does not answer the questions with an uneqivocal yes or no. He rather answered them,

> "Go and tell John what you hear and see: the blind receive their sight and the lame walk, lepers are cleansed and the deaf hear, and the dead are raised up, and the poor have good news preached to them. And blessed is he who takes no offense at me" (Matthew 11:4–6).

Why this cryptic answer? Because he was quoting from the Old Testament! Isaiah (29:18–19; 35:5–6; 61:1; as well as Luke 4:18, 19) was speaking of the age to come when God would send the Messiah to the world. Jesus was claiming this heritage.

The other occasion is in the final chapter of Luke. After Jesus was risen from the dead he addressed his disciples and indicated that "these are my words which I spoke to you, while I was still with you, that everything written about me in the law of Moses and the prophets and the psalms must be fulfilled" (Luke 24:44). Jesus stated that he was the One expected in the Old Testament.

Karl Barth helped us to view the Old Testament through eyes that are enlightened by Christian faith. Barth argued that Jesus is the ultimate revelation of God, and that this high point of revelation governs the entire history of divine revelation. Moreover, the pre-existent Christ participated in the revelation recorded in the Old Testament. Bernard Ramm explained:

> Barth understands the pre-existence of Christ (as he appears in the Old Testament), the incarnation, the crucifixion, the resurrection, the ascension, the heavenly reign, and the return of Christ to be one event. They are not one event in the sense of happening at the same time. Rather, each event implicates the other events in such a manner that no one event can be separated from any other. They are a unified sequence that cannot suffer division.
>
> A famous preacher was asked what he felt about the second coming. His reply was that he was so busy preaching about the first coming he has not come around to preaching on the second coming. According to Barth, this is an idiotic remark. Unless there is a second coming of Christ, the first coming hangs suspended with no purpose, no goal, no *telos*.[2]

Gerhard von Rad, noted Old Testament theologian, saw the Old Testament as foreshadowing what the early Christians found in Jesus Christ. Just as the Word of God became action in the Old

Testament, maintained von Rad, so the Word of God became flesh in the New Testament.

We can even see that the Old Testament words had become something of a habit in Jesus' thinking and speaking. Recall his temptation in the desert. He was pressured to achieve God's purposes by the devil's means. He responded to each temptation with words from the Old Testament. At the point of testing and distress, he was able to come forth almost automatically with words of Scripture. He spoke similarly on the cross. Even in the midst of his agony and the almost unconscious speaking of his deepest feelings, Jesus used biblical language.

Although Jesus recognized the authority of the Old Testament, he did not regard this authority the same way as he regarded the authority of the religious teachers of his day. The most popular of these teachers were the Pharisees and the scribes. These men considered it their responsibility to guard the truth of the Scriptures. They applied these Scriptures in specific areas of life and told the people how to obey certain interpretations of biblical rules and standards. Thus they accepted not only the authority of the Scriptures but the authority of the interpretations that had been made by various teachers. Jesus refused to recognize these traditions as being on the same level as the Old Testament.

Jesus did more than recognize the authority of the Old Testament. He indicated that he had come to fulfill its teachings. Consider his well-known words as they are recorded early in the Sermon on the Mount:

> "Think not that I have come to abolish the law and the prophets; I have come not to abolish them but to fulfil them. For truly, I say to you, till heaven and earth pass away, not an iota, not a dot, will pass from the law until all is accomplished" (Matthew 5:17-18).

These words of Jesus reflect both of the basic relationships that he had with the Old Testament. It is obvious that he accepted the authority of the Old Testament. He did not come to abolish the law and the prophets. But he did not recognize this authority as static. He came to fulfill the Old Testament. On the one hand, nothing will be lost; nothing will be destroyed. On the other hand, all will be fulfilled. So he maintained all the central teachings of the Old Testament, yet also carried them forward to their ultimate meaning and purpose. This fulfilling of the Old Testament is bringing to fruition that which is central and implicit within the meaning of the Scriptures. Just as the butterfly is the fulfillment of the caterpillar; just as the oak tree is the fulfillment of the acorn; so Jesus both in his being and in his teaching was the fulfillment of the Old Testament. He sensed, as did Handel the composer, that he was the personification of these prophetic words of Isaiah:

> For to us a child is born,
>   to us a son is given;
> and the government will be upon his shoulder,
>   and his name will be called
> "Wonderful Counselor, Mighty God,
>   Everlasting Father, Prince of Peace."
>   —Isaiah 9:6

Jesus did not destroy what was in the Old Testament; he rather brought it to what it was meant to be.

Jesus—Teacher of the Old Testament

In the process of fulfilling the Old Testament Jesus taught in a manner that was significantly different from that of the scribal teachers with whom the Jewish people were familiar. Mark states that "they were astonished at his teaching, for he taught them as one who had authority, and not as the scribes" (Mark 1:22). The scribes simply stated what the Old Testament said. Then they quoted the rabbinic teachers (including their varied disagreements) as they had spoken to particular concerns. Jesus, on the contrary, avoided the quotations of all the revered authorities. He stated the Old Testament teaching and then moved to the heart of the matter. He was interested in the original meaning and the purpose of God as reflected in the Old Testament. He spoke as a prophet who said, "Thus says the Lord!"

There were two elements in Jesus' teaching that made him different from the scribes. First, he saw the ideals that God demanded in the Old Testament and refused to encrust these ideals in specific rules. He understood the Old Testament as the prophet Jeremiah expressed it. "I will put my law within them, and I will write it upon their hearts; and I will be their God, and they shall be my people" (Jeremiah 31:33). Jesus saw Scripture as the ideal teaching of God that would be written in the hearts of those who believe. It would not be the fearful following of minute regulations, but the radical response of a people committed to God.

Ideas reduced to regulations become encrusted legalisms. Legalisms, in turn, contain loopholes. Hollywood tradition includes the following conversation:

MAE WEST: "What's an old reprobate like you doing reading the Bible?"

W. C. FIELDS: "Just looking for loopholes, Mae, just looking for loopholes!"

Our humorous reflections upon legalisms in more churchly circles include the conversation of the Roman Catholic priest and the Jewish rabbi:

"Say, Rabbi, now that we Catholics can eat meat on Fridays, when will you Jews be able to eat pork?"

"At your wedding, Father!"

The issue has been expressed more effectively by the late Helmut Thielicke of the University of Hamburg:

The Christian stands, not under the dictatorship of a legalistic 'You ought,' but in the magnetic field of Christian freedom, under the empowering of the 'You may.'

Jesus' concern with Scripture as the ideal teaching of God and his rejection of legalistic formulations became basic to the thinking of the early Christian church. Professor F. F. Bruce finds four great themes emphasized in the teachings of Paul that are still needed today. First and foremost, he says:

True religion is not a matter of rules and regulations. God does not deal with people like an accountant, but accepts them freely when they respond to His love, and implants the Spirit of Christ in their hearts so that they may show to others the love they have received from Him.[3]

Second, Jesus held that the motive of a person was as important, or even more important, than some specific act. Attitude, motivation, desire—these are important before God who can see the depths of our hearts. Soren Kierkegaard asks the question: "Is charitable intent essential to an act of charity or mercy?" He answers his own question with an imaginative recounting of a Gospel narrative:

> Take the story about the woman who placed the two pennies in the temple treasury, but let us poetise a little variation. The two pennies were for her a great sum, which she had not quickly accumulated. She had saved for a long time in order to get them saved up, and then she had hidden them wrapped in a little cloth in order to bring them when she herself went up to the temple. But a swindler had detected that she possessed this money, had tricked her out of it, and had exchanged the cloth for an identical piece which was utterly empty— something which the widow did not know. Thereupon she went up to the temple, placed as she intended, the two pennies, that is nothing, in the temple treasury: I wonder if Christ would not still have said what he said of her that 'she gave more than all the rich'?[4]

Jesus drove deeper into the meaning of the Old Testament than did his contemporaries. He expanded the teaching of Scripture; he did not deny it.

This practice is most clear in Matthew 5. There Jesus referred, among other things, to the sixth commandment, "You shall not kill" (Matthew 5:21); the seventh commandment, "You shall not commit adultery" (Matthew 5:27); and the regulation about swearing (Matthew 5:33). Note Jesus' teachings concerning each of these matters with a view to seeing how he emphasized the importance of internal motives as well as external acts.

Jesus' audience all agreed, as we do, that murder is wrong. So did Jesus. Jesus, however, pointed out that murder as an act began with hatred as a motive.

"You have heard that it was said to the men of old, 'You shall not kill; and whoever kills shall be liable to judgment.' But I say to you that every one who is angry with his brother shall be liable to judgment" (Matthew 5:21, 22).

We should look to our inner motives and to God's ultimate ideals. God doesn't want us to desire to kill or even to hate. The seed of hatred may develop into the fruit of murder.

Jesus continued by indicating that the same understanding should be applied to the seventh commandment, the statement against adultery. It is not only the act of adultery but also the desire for an adulterous relationship that is wrong. Just as the seed of murder is hatred, so the seed of adultery is the lustful look, the licentious desire. "You have heard that it was said, 'You shall not commit adultery.' But I say to you that every one who looks at a woman lustfully has already committed adultery with her in his heart" (Matthew 5:27, 28). We should be concerned not only with the rules with which we limit ourselves to legal and proper relationships. We should also be concerned with the ideals of God who sees deep within our hearts. This does not mean that we should commit the overt act of murder or adultery simply because we have experienced the feeling of hatred or lust. It means, rather, that we should seek God's ideal in both act and attitude.

Jesus also referred to the Old Testament command not to swear by the name of God falsely. Some interpreters of this passage indicated that one might legally swear by some item other than the name of God. The rule only referred to God's name, they said. But Jesus drove back to the need for an inner ideal of truth. "Do not swear at all," he said (Matthew 5:34a). His concern was not to avoid an oath. Instead, he proposed that we should tell the truth. He did not tell us to refrain from an oath in a courtroom. He said we should refrain from lying. Thus, Jesus continued, "Let what you say be simply 'Yes' or 'No'; anything more than this comes from evil" (Matthew 5:37). We should not need misleading oaths to impress those whom we try to confuse. Any desire to make a falsehood seem more true grows out of a desire to deceive. Hence it comes from evil!

This discussion suggests that Jesus did not deny the Old Testament. He rather interpreted it with a view to getting at the original and basic purposes of God. God's purpose has to do with our inner being and motivation. These states, as well as our actions, should conform to the will of God.

The divine concern for our inner needs is reflected on several occasions when Jesus confronted the religious leaders and their demand for proper cleansing and rituals before eating. Jesus indi-

cated that God is not nearly so concerned about the details of external cleansing as with the essential honesty of the heart.

This same concern (for our essential motivation) is reflected in
Jesus' arguments with religious leaders about the sabbath, the day
of rest. Jesus indicated that we should not be slaves to the rule about
a day of complete rest. If a task needed to be done for the good of
one of God's creatures, the task should be performed.

> "What man of you, if he has one sheep and it falls into a pit on the
> sabbath, will not lay hold of it and lift it out? Of how much more
> value is a man than a sheep! So it is lawful to do good on the sabbath"
> (Matthew 12:11, 12).

The important thing is not to codify the rule about not working
on the sabbath. It is proper to do a good thing even on the day of
rest.

By the way of summary, we should remember that Jesus recognized the authority of the Old Testament. It was his Bible, and it
was the Bible of his first followers. He was extremely familiar with
the Scriptures. He developed the pattern for his own life and ministry from them. He saw himself as the One toward whom Scripture
pointed. His teachings were deeply immersed in the Old Testament, but he was not bound by the interpretations of previous and
prevailing religious leaders. Jesus saw the Scripture as more than a
book of rules. It was the living Word of God. He saw himself as
fulfilling the biblical message and the Old Testament as the ideal
teaching of God, not a series of regulations to be slavishly followed.

Thus, our attitudes and motives are important, even as are our
acts. God knows our deepest thoughts as well as our doings.

Jesus' entire life was one of emphasis upon a sense of personal
relationship with God. He sensed that he was God's son, and
wanted all to become God's children.

God is not a cruel taskmaster who demands our response to limitless regulations. We are not to approach God with a sense of fear.
Nor are we to stand before others with a need of proving our goodness. God seeks us out as children. We are to accept the fact that we
are accepted. God wants us to love, even as we are loved. Then we
are to live freely and gladly. We are to see and to seek the purposes

of God within individual experience and in all relationships.

The gospel presents these ideals not as demands that we must achieve, but as the new life and nature that we express. "As an apple-tree does not produce apples by Act of Parliament, but because it is its nature to do so, the character of Christ cannot be produced in his people by rules and regulations; it must be the fruit of his Spirit within them."[5]

These spirit-filled ideals are the power of the gospel for Christian living. They were the essence of Jesus' life and the heart of what he taught. They are also, Jesus said, the message of the Old Testament.

Chapter Ten

God's People: Jews or Gentiles?

The Teachings of Jesus Concerning the Chosen People

W hat did Jesus look like? When asked that question, what image is reflected in your mind? Is it a painting which you have seen? Is it a particular actor whom you saw portraying the role?

Many still see Jesus as a white Protestant of the twentieth century. He reflects what some consider to be the best of our middle class culture—grey flannel suit, influential position, fine family, suburban home, station wagon, and all the trimmings! This is the type of man, in many instances, who is recognized as a Christian gentleman. Thus, it is not strange that many assume Jesus to be like that.

The fact is that Jesus was a Jew. The Jewishness of Jesus is initially surprising to some. Professor Pierson Parker, of the General Theological Seminary, told the following story to the Society of Biblical Literature:

> A Baptist minister went to heaven and was told by St. Peter that he would have a Volkswagen for his use. The minister was pleased until he noticed a Catholic priest driving a Cadillac. When he complained, St. Peter explained that the priest had to give up having a wife and children when he was on earth and therefore was entitled to a luxury car. The minister then understood and went on his way. Sev-

eral hours later, however, he saw a rabbi driving a Rolls Royce. He rushed to St. Peter and said, "I'm willing to admit that the priest had to give up a wife and children and deserved to have a Cadillac. But what about the rabbi? He had a wife and children." "That's true," said St. Peter. "But remember—he's a relative of the boss."

Or witness this argument: "All right, all right! I'll admit that Jesus was Jewish. But at least his mother was a Catholic!"

Jesus was Jewish. He never really left his homeland, and the twelve persons who were closest to him were all Jewish. Even so, they didn't look like your Jewish friend down the street. The disciples were a ruddy lot—brown-skinned, hardened, of the outdoor type. The people with whom they associated and among whom they ministered were, in large measure, of the same stripe.

The Jews of Jesus' day had an illustrious history. They were determinative in the history of the ancient Near East far beyond their numbers. God had spoken to some of the outstanding leaders in their past. They had become the heirs of a great spiritual deposit. In their own society, the Jews were far from a despised minority. On the contrary, they saw themselves as the people of God.

With reference to the Jewish people as God's chosen, N. W. Ewer has presented a now famous epigram.

> HOW ODD
> OF GOD
> TO CHOOSE
> THE JEWS.

Two answers have been offered in rebuttal to this epigram. The first is simply explanatory:

> NOW NEWS
> NOT ODD,
> THE JEWS
> CHOSE GOD.

The second is presented in the same tone as Ewer's:

> NOT ODD
> OF GOD,
> THE GOYIM (Gentiles)
> ANNOY HIM.

Conscious of their calling as God's Chosen People, the Jews developed a sense of justifiable pride. Unfortunately this pride sometimes evolved into exclusivism and snobbishness.

The elite of the ancient Jewish society considered and treated non-Jews as outcasts. We all have a way of dividing society into two simple groups—our own group and the outsiders. The outsiders are often referred to with generalizations and even sneers. The Greeks saw only two groups in society, themselves and the "barbarians." Modern Moslems see only themselves and the "infidels." We Christians see only ourselves and the "outsiders" or the "lost." And these Jews saw only themselves and the "Gentiles." Often they were referred to as "Gentile dogs" (as in Matthew 15:26; Mark 7:27; Philippians 3:2).

This all too common human activity of rejecting the "outsiders" may reflect different motives. Conservative social units, for example, are slow to accept others into the group. A Virginian told about a trip to Vermont and a visit with a friend, a fifth–generation Vermonter. One evening they heard on the news that the 1980 census recorded over a half–million Vermonters. "Not true," said the Vermonter. "Most of those people just live here!"

In many tribal societies one refuses to relate to anyone outside the family. Albert Schweitzer observed this in his work at Lambarene. He noted that primitive people related in solidarity only with members of the same tribe. When Schweitzer asked a patient to help a fellow patient, the patient would agree only if the other belonged to the same tribe. Otherwise, the reply would be, "This is not brother for me." Nothing would change this way of thinking.

Unfortunately, our rejection of others often reflects an inappropriate and unwarranted sense of superiority. In his typical manner, Mark Twain spoke to this human foible when he said,

> I'm quite sure that . . . I have no race prejudices, and I think I have no color prejudices nor creed prejudices. Indeed, I know it. I can stand any society. All I care to know is that a man is a human being—that is enough for me; he can't be any worse.

First-century Jews saw outsiders as either Gentile or partially Gentile. The Samaritans, who were partly Jewish, are a good example. When the people of Palestine were deported by their Assyrian conquerors some eight centuries before, only the unskilled laborers and their peasant families were left in the land. (This uprooting of people and moving them to a different land has been practiced in our century by Adolph Hitler.) The Samaritan people resulted from the intermarriage between Gentiles and Jews as a result of this uprooting. The modern Samaritans and their ancestors are in many ways Jewish. They recognize the Old Testament Scriptures. They look back with pride to the great patriarchs of the Jewish people—Abraham, Isaac, Jacob—as their own spiritual forebears. But they were rejected by strict Jews (as mentioned in John 4:9).

The small modern Samaritan community lives at peace with its Jewish neighbors under the protection of Israeli law. The contemporary Jewish community, both in America and elsewhere, generally exerts leadership in the area of religious liberty and racial respect. As Christians, we must continue to unite with the children of Abraham in preventing any future holocaust.

Indeed, Christian faith calls us to accept all people. This concern is more than courtesy, although true courtesy is universal. As George Bernard Shaw's Professor Higgins said,

> "The great secret, Eliza, is not having bad manners or good manners, or any other particular sort of manners, but having the same manners for all human souls: in short, behaving as if you were in Heaven, where there are no third–class carriages, and one soul is as good as another."[1]

The biblical concern is deeper. Professor F. F. Bruce verbalized the theme in this way: "Unfair discrimination on the grounds of race, religion, class or sex is an offense against God and humanity alike."[2]

Christians have not always succeeded in rejecting racism. Nevertheless, we have not always failed. Elton Trueblood reflected:

> After all the familiar criticisms have been leveled at the existent churches, the fact remains that periods of crisis often reveal real differences between the Church and the surrounding world. . . . A striking example of this was provided during the late war, when American citizens were forcibly removed from their home in Pacific Coast

states because they were of Japanese ancestry. All are now enabled to know how exceedingly unjust and how unnecessary this action was, inasmuch as the Congressional inquiry has failed to find a single authenticated case of sabotage by these people. Many suffered severe economic loss, disruption of careers and of schooling, in addition to the psychological harm of being treated as third-class citizens. A large proportion of our population know this now, but the point is that those who knew it at the time, and had the courage to say so, were people whose idealism had been mediated to them through the fellowship which began long ago in the mind of Christ. A representative body of Japanese-Americans has recently reported to their amazement that all the people who helped them in relocation or education or care of property were acting from definite Christian inspiration. *The patriotic societies did not help them, but the Christians did.* Such an example is good to remember when criticism is most sweeping and vicious.[3]

Jesus' Ministry to Jews

How did Jesus feel about this issue? Were the Jewish people superior to the other nations? Did he recognize values and spiritual insights among the Samaritans? Did he serve among the people of the entire world, or were his teachings directed only toward his Jewish neighbors?

We may be somewhat surprised when we analyze Jesus' views on these issues. We, naturally, expect him to be broad in his interests and to be accepting of all peoples. We assume that he treated all people equally and carried his ministry to Jews and non-Jews without discrimination. But there are evidences that he did not.

Consider the account of Jesus sending his twelve disciples on a special preaching mission. His words of instruction were these: "Go nowhere among the Gentiles, and enter no town of the Samaritans, but go rather to the lost sheep of the house of Israel" (Matthew 10:5, 6).

Or recall the time when Jesus was moving to the northeastern portion of Palestine with his own disciples. He came into the general area of the ancient Phoenicians near the cities of Tyre and Sidon. A woman who was desperately concerned for her daughter approached Jesus and asked for help. This particular woman was non-Jewish. We may be somewhat shocked with the way Jesus spoke to her. After her entreaty, Matthew's record of Jesus' response is this:

> But he did not answer her a word. And his disciples came and begged him, saying "Send her away, for she is crying after us." He answered, "I was sent only to the lost sheep of the house of Israel." But she came and knelt before him, saying "Lord, help me." And he answered, "It is not fair to take the children's bread and throw it to the dogs." She said, "Yes, Lord, yet even the dogs eat the crumbs that fall from their master's table." Then Jesus answered her, "O woman, great is your faith! Be it done for you as you desire." And her daughter was healed instantly (Matthew 15:23–28).

We are relieved to see that her request was finally granted, but are puzzled by the words of Jesus: "I was sent only to the lost sheep of the house of Israel;" "It is not fair to take the children's bread and throw it to the dogs."

Does God play favorites? If we only listen to Jesus' words on these two occasions, we might well feel the answer is in the affirmative. Our immediate response to Jesus' statement on these occasions might be that he has no concern for non-Jews. To be sure, we sense that this seems contradictory to the general spirit of Jesus' actions and words. But do we have records of his teachings that indicate interest beyond the Jewish people?

A Testimony to All Nations

Examples of Jesus' ministry to the Gentiles are not wanting. The first passage to which we referred was Jesus' words to the disciples when he was sending them out on a preaching mission. On this specific occasion his words included these: "You will be dragged before governors and kings for my sake, to bear testimony before them and the Gentiles" (Matthew 10:18). Rather than ignoring the non-Jews, the disciples are "to bear testimony before them."

In this same Gospel, there are two other occasions in which Jesus speaks of a ministry to non-Jews. In Matthew 24, Jesus speaks to his disciples on the Mount of Olives just outside the city of Jerusalem. He tells them of things to come. Among other things he says, "And this gospel of the kingdom will be preached throughout the whole world, as a testimony to all nations . . ." (Matthew 24:14). Rather than being limited to the Jewish hearers, the Good

News will go to *all* nations. Matthew's Gospel closes with Jesus' statement to his disciples that has been called the "Great Commission." Consider the universality of these words: "Go therefore and make disciples of *all* nations . . . and, lo, I am with you always, to the close of the age" (Matthew 28:19, 20, author's emphasis).

Beyond these specific statements of Jesus, there are many hints of his interest in people outside the Jewish nation. Recall the story of the good Samaritan. This title, which we attribute to the story, is enough to indicate Jesus' lack of narrow Jewish concern. The hero in the story was a *good* Samaritan. When two Jewish religious leaders who were exceptionally righteous and pious passed by a needy person, it was a Samaritan who showed concern and acted as a neighbor. Then there was the time when Jesus healed ten lepers. Only one of them returned to give thanks. His nationality? Luke tells us that he was a Samaritan (Luke 17:16).

Now we see both sides of the coin. An initial glance at Jesus' words and actions might indicate that he was only concerned about his Jewish neighbors. On other occasions, however, it becomes clear that he was—and is—concerned about Gentiles and Samaritans as well. How are we to determine whether he thought of his own people as superior? The answer is to be found in serious consideration of at least two significant acts of Jesus in behalf of needy people outside the Jewish community.

Although the evidence seems to point in two directions, we must consider it all the same. Otherwise, our prejudices may be reflected in premature closure and inappropriate conclusions on the basis of inadequate evidence. Daniel Boorstin was correct in observing, "The greatest obstacle to discovering the shape of the earth, the continents and the ocean was not ignorance but the illusion of knowledge."

(Sydney Harris described to his son how he went from Detroit to Windsor, Canada, by going south. His son could not believe him. Harris then wrote a syndicated column on "Maps of the Mind." Reno is west of Los Angeles; Jacksonville is west of Cleveland. Go south far enough, and the sun rises in the Pacific while setting in the Atlantic. Our generalizations and conclusions should await all of the evidence.)

The Centurion's Slave

In observing Jesus' concern for needy non-Jews, let us examine first the healing of the centurion's slave (Matthew 8:5-13; Luke 7:1-10). The event takes place in the city of Capernaum. This was the community out of which Jesus worked during most of his ministry. He moved to Capernaum from his hometown of Nazareth. Capernaum is located on the northern edge of the Lake of Galilee, and it is a lovely area of rolling hills from which the lake is visible.

Luke describes the occasion:

> Now a centurion had a slave who was dear to him, who was sick and at the point of death. When he heard of Jesus, he sent to him elders of the Jews, asking him to come and heal his slave. And when they came to Jesus, they besought him earnestly, saying, "He is worthy to have you do this for him, for he loves our nation, and he built us our synagogue." And Jesus went with them. When he was not far from the house, the centurion sent friends to him, saying to him, "Lord, do not trouble yourself, for I am not worthy to have you come under my roof; therefore I did not presume to come to you. But say the word, and let my servant be healed. For I am a man set under authority, with soldiers under me: and I say to one, 'Go,' and he goes; and to another, 'Come,' and he comes; and to my slave, 'Do this,' and he does it." When Jesus heard this he marveled at him, and turned and said to the multitude that followed him, "I tell you, not even in Israel have I found such faith." And when those who had been sent returned to the house, they found the slave well (Luke 7:2–10).

We can sense both Jesus' and Luke's attitude toward this man as we read the preceding account. The attitudes of Jesus and Luke reflect the feelings of early Christians in general toward this type of non-Jew. The things we note are all in the centurion's favor.

First, he was concerned about his slave. This was unusual among the Romans. A slave was considered an animal. Slaves were without human rights. A master could take a slave's life and no questions were asked. But this centurion reflected a genuine devotion to the slave who served him.

Second, he was a man of genuine commitment to the God of Israel. The Jews spoke highly of him; he had built a synagogue for them.

Third, he was a man of humility. He felt unworthy to come into

Jesus' presence. Similarly, he felt unworthy to have Jesus enter his home. Although he might have been proud of his gift of a synagogue for the Jews and might have expected recognition from them, he knew that a strict Jew should not enter the home of a Gentile. Inasmuch as it was his Jewish friends who spoke to Jesus, it is likely that this man had asked them to do so in order that he might not embarrass Jesus. Little did he realize that Jesus would be interested in him as a person created by God. Jesus would not reject him simply because of his race. Mistaken though he was, the centurion was a man of genuine modesty and humility.

Finally, and most importantly, the centurion exemplified outstanding faith. He assumed that Jesus had power greater than his own and even equal to that of God. As he, himself, had the ability to order things done apart from his immediate personal activity, he was strong enough in faith to believe that Jesus could do the same at a miraculous level. Jesus was impressed. "I tell you," he said, "not even in Israel have I found such faith."

The Demon–Possessed Daughter

The other outstanding act of Jesus for a non-Jew is recorded by Matthew (Matthew 15:21–28). This event reflects a time in the latter portion of Jesus' ministry. He had concluded his work among the multitudes in Galilee, and was moving to the outer reaches of Palestine. It seems that he was seeking some relief from the pressing crowds. He wanted some time for privacy and meditation. He also wanted to spend more of his time in instructing his own disciples. Among other things, Jesus was likely pondering the question as to where the main thrust of his ministry should be. Should he extend himself to non-Jews, or should he continue preaching exclusively in the Jewish community? In this situation, a non-Jewish woman approached him.

> And Jesus went away from there and withdrew to the district of Tyre and Sidon. And behold, a Canaanite woman from that region came out and cried, "Have mercy on me, O Lord, Son of David; my daughter is severely possessed by a demon." But he did not answer her a word. And his disciples came and begged him, saying, "Send her away, for she is crying after us." He answered, "I was sent only to

the lost sheep of the house of Israel." But she came and knelt before him, saying, "Lord, help me." And he answered, "It is not fair to take the children's bread and throw it to the dogs." She said, "Yes, Lord, yet even the dogs eat the crumbs that fall from their master's table." Then Jesus answered her, "O woman, great is your faith! Be it done for you as you desire." And her daughter was healed instantly (Matthew 15:21–28).

Two problems jump out in this passage. One is Jesus' statement in verse 24: "I was sent only to the lost sheep of the house of Israel." This is similar to his statement to the twelve disciples when he sent them out on their preaching mission. They were to go not to "Gentiles, and . . . Samaritans, but . . . rather to the lost sheep of the house of Israel" (Matthew 10:5, 6). The former statement seems almost cruel. He said to the woman, "It is not fair to take the children's bread and throw it to the dogs" (Matthew 15:26). Did Jesus think of Gentiles as dogs? Was he interested only in Jews? How can we relate the attitude reflected here to the benevolent attitude Jesus held in the rest of his ministry?

We should remember that the Gospel of Mark was written before Matthew. The earlier Gospel reflected the words of Jesus more fully. Mark states that Jesus said to the woman, "Let the children first be fed, for it is not right to take the children's bread and throw it to the dogs" (Mark 7:27). The word "first" is important. Jesus was not excluding non-Jews, but emphasizing the priority of ministry among the Jews. We should also notice that the woman felt some encouragement even in the midst of this rebuff by Jesus. When Jesus mentioned dogs, he seemed to do it as a method of encouraging her further. She felt justified in pressing her request and saying, "Yes, Lord, yet even the dogs eat the crumbs that fall from their master's table." This combination of faith and humility was adequate. Her request was granted.

Unfortunately for us, this story—like so many in the Gospels—is in summary form. We do not have any description of the overtones expressed in Jesus' comments. Nor can we see the facial expressions that may have given a turn to the meaning of his words. Was he rejecting this Gentile woman harshly? Or was he gently, even playfully, encouraging her in the midst of her concern? Or was he reflecting, and possibly even mocking, the attitude of his disciples who asked him to send her away? He may have been speaking to the woman with tongue–in–cheek only to show the disciples how narrow, hardhearted, and churlish were their attitudes. In any case, she rose to the occasion most ably. Her faith was great, and her need was met.

Even Jesus had no simple way of handling the prejudice of his disciples. Facts do not necessarily change feelings. Oliver Wendell Holmes was right in observing: "The mind of the bigot is like the pupil of the eye. The more light you pour upon it, the more it will contract."

Before trying to understand the primary thrust of the stories of the healing of the centurion's servant and the Syrophoenician woman's daughter, we should notice some unique elements in these stories. First, and foremost, these two non-Jewish persons who approached Jesus reflected the kind of faith and confidence in his ability that was not reflected elsewhere, even among Jews.

Second, both of these healings were done at a distance. The immediate presence—much less the touch—of Jesus was unnecessary for these healings. It is interesting, and perhaps important, to note that these are the only healings that Jesus did at a distance.

Third, these Gentile persons only received. They did not join the disciples in order to learn and serve. They were those who received without uniting with the apostolic band. This approach did not reflect the primary goal of Jesus' ministry. He wanted not only those who were seeking, but those who, having found, would be serving. He wanted a depth of relationship that would continue in fellowship with him for the service of God.

This leads us to conclude that Jesus met these needs simply because they were needs. The primary thrust and purpose of his ministry was to relate people to God so they could continue a service and relationship to others for years to come. This is likely the reason he limited himself primarily to his own people. Similarly, he gave most of his teaching to a dozen disciples. Is this not the reason why Jesus was most often interested only in Jewish people, while on other occasions he was interested in non-Jews as well? He wanted to relate to those who were closest so that they could relate to others.

Jesus did not teach or act as if God played favorites. He did not support any superiority of the Jews. Rather, he stressed a priority in his own ministry.

We can summarize this chapter with two statements. First, Jesus taught and lived a Jewish priority, but not a Jewish favoritism. Second, the main thrust of Jesus' teachings and doings is that the Gentiles would be reached through Jews. The Jews are first, but this chronology reflects not so much favoritism as responsibility and strategy. Jesus began with a few who were close at home, but he wanted to reach the many—even at the end of the world.

Does this not say something to us who are Christians today? We are to carry the Good News of God's love "to all nations." It does not mean, necessarily, that we begin at the end of the world. It means that we begin with that person next door. It means talking to that co-worker. It means reaching out to the friend in the classroom. It means witnessing to that hardest one, closest to us. Some, of course, will minister to those who are distant. The one near is the priority for most of us, but reaching everyone is a necessity.

Father, who has made all men in thy likeness, and lovest all whom thou has made, suffer not our family to separate itself from thee by building barriers of race and color. As thy Son our Saviour was born of a Hebrew mother, but rejoiced in the faith of a Syrian woman and of a Roman soldier, welcomed the Greeks who sought him, and suffered a man from Africa to carry his cross, so teach us to regard the members of all races as fellow heirs of the kingdom of Jesus Christ our Lord.

(A prayer for racial harmony attributed to Olive Warner).

Chapter Eleven

Are We Responsible for Others?

The Teachings of Jesus Concerning Social Service

"A m I my brother's keeper?" The question is an old one. It is found in the first book of the Bible. Adam and Eve had several children. The first two were boys named Cain and Abel. Cain killed his brother Abel. After the murder God asked Cain, "Where is Abel your brother?" Cain's retort: "I do not know; am I my brother's keeper?" (Genesis 4:9). So the question was originally a dodge. For some, it is still a dodge. The language of relationship, and even of piety, is used to avoid social responsibility.

The question, however, remains a worthy one. "Am I my brother's keeper?" Do I act responsibly toward others? Or do I live entirely to myself? Modern–day North Americans used to emphasize rugged individualism. Now we realize that the world is becoming increasingly one. There is nothing that happens on the other side of the globe that does not, in some measure, affect each of us.

Our interdependence has been dramatically emphasized by John Donne, seventeenth–century Dean of St. Paul's Cathedral in London. Anticipating his own imminent death he wrote:

No man is an island, entire of itself; every man is a piece of the continent, a part of the main. If a clod be washed away by the sea, Europe is the less as well as if a promontory were, as well as if a manor of thy friend's or if thine own were; any man's death diminishes me, because I am involved in mankind, and therefore never send to know for whom the bell tolls; it tolls for thee.[1]

John Donne would say, "Yes—I am my brother's keeper!"

But what would Jesus say? Again, an unequivocal "yes!" Consider his words: "So if you are offering your gift at the altar, and there remember that your brother has something against you, leave your gift . . ." (Matthew 5:23–24a). So I am responsible for my brothers and sisters. Even if I am worshiping almighty God and remember that someone has something against me, I should withhold my worship temporarily until the relationship is reestablished. Nothing is more important than the relationship with another, Jesus said, not even worship in the midst of estrangement. Without question, I bear responsibility for others.

Educators tell us that learning takes place in ways different from our expectations. Most of us seem to feel that we learn when we pick up some new fact. But learning is now being defined as a measurable change in the learner. Thus, learning is more than facts. We acquire new skills. We develop certain attitudes. When we learn we become different. A measurable change takes place.

Such change is often slower than anticipated or desired, particularly when it represents social or group learning. Large bodies, including church congregations and denominations, move slowly. This phenomenon is especially true in the free church tradition, inasmuch as change should result from persuasion and consensus rather than from the exercise of authority and power.

Slowness to change is less excusable in authoritative structures such as the State. It is widely known that Americans refer to British naval personnel as "limeys" or lime–juicers. This is because the British navy endorses the consumption of lime juice as a nutritional substitute. The origin of this practice is not so well known. A British sea captain noted that the sailors under his command who consumed lime juice were free from scurvy. He reported this to the admiralty. It was twenty years before the admiralty tested the use of lime juice as an antiscorbutic on another boat. It was successful.

Then it was another hundred years before the practice was instituted for the rest of the fleet!

How would the concept of learning as measurable change relate to the learning offered to us by Jesus, the master teacher? Quite positively. When Jesus taught it was in order that we might be different. He taught with a view to bringing his followers to a personal or social decision.

When we ask what Jesus taught about relating our lives and specific behaviors to a given decision, we are asking what Jesus taught about ethics. Indeed, he taught much about ethical behavior. This teaching was not presented in a systematic fashion. It was not developed from basic philosophical premises or expressed through syllogisms. A Christian life–style grows directly out of the will of God and comes to us in terms that demand decisions. If we really learn from Jesus, we are significantly changed. If we only hear his words and are not deeply affected, we have not become his disciples, true learners.

If we are to learn from our Lord, then, we should concentrate upon that which is most important. What is the heart of Jesus' life and teachings? What was the basic reason for his coming, living, teaching? I think he summarized it best himself in a twofold statement: "For the Son of man also came not to be served but to serve, and to give his life as a ransom for many" (Mark 10:45). "Serve" is translated "to minister" in the older translations of the Bible. That is because the minister is essentially a servant of the people. But the word "serve" more clearly communicates the idea to us. So the two main thrusts of Jesus' ministry were to serve and to give his life. Most of us underscore one or another of these emphases. Jesus drew them both together.

Some of us emphasize Jesus' sacrifice in the giving of his life to the point of denying his serving. We emphasize Jesus' interest in individual souls. We underscore his concern with the spiritual, and play down any emphasis upon social problems. But Jesus had much to say about social concerns. He was deeply concerned about the poor and oppressed. He was interested in every area of human life. To respond to Jesus at a spiritual level is to commit also the physical and social arenas of our existence to him. We must remember his teaching that our service to the needy is a spiritual service to Jesus himself (Matthew 25:34–40).

The failure or refusal of some Christians to uphold both of these emphases led E. Stanley Jones to comment: "An individual gospel without a social gospel is a soul without a body and a social gospel without an individual gospel is a body without a soul. One is a ghost and the other is a corpse."[2]

When Dr. Alan Walter was addressing the Methodist Conference of South Africa in 1981, he commented: "There is no greater menace in the church than a born–again Christian without a social conscience. But I am also convinced that the social activist Christian without a personal experience and commitment to Christ is as great a menace."

This unwarranted division of the biblical concern for the individual as well as our life together was anticipated by some of our more insightful Christian leaders. When Dr. Walter E. Woodbury offered his first annual report (in 1937) as the new Director of Evangelism for American Baptist Churches in the U.S.A. he said, "We are . . . encouraging our pastors and churches to have done with the fiction of salvation for disembodied spirits, apart from real redemption of the total personality, body, mind and soul."[3]

While some will emphasize Jesus' death without reference to service, others will emphasize Jesus' serving and accordingly play down his giving of his life. Jesus is thereby a teacher and a social reformer, but not Lord and Savior. Now we may have a right to this viewpoint, but we should never claim that it comes from the New Testament! The Gospel accounts of Jesus' life are extremely clear at this point. He was far more than a social reformer. Indeed, this was the essence of the temptations through which Jesus went (Matthew 4:1–11; Luke 4:1–13). He was tempted to do the work of a great teacher and social reformer, but in a way that would be unworthy of the Lord and Savior who he came to be. The fact is, there is not much in the way of strictly social ethics in the Gospels. Jesus does not teach us specifically how to relate to the community at large, to political systems, or to the economic order. Rather, he confronts us with the demands of God upon our experience. We must then relate to him as we consider our relationship to our sisters and brothers and the social situations about us.

This call has led Mother Teresa to remonstrate, "I can't bear the pain when people call me a social worker. My life is devoted to Christ; it is for him that I breathe and see. Had I been a social worker I'd have left it long ago." Speaking for her Sisters of Charity, she says: "We are not social workers, we are not nurses, we are not teachers, we are religious." When a brother said, "My vocation is to work for the lepers," Mother Teresa corrected: "You are making a mistake, Brother; your vocation is to belong to Jesus. He has chosen you for himself, and the work you do is only a means to express your love to him in action."[4]

Much can be said about the ethical teachings of Jesus, but we shall endeavor to summarize these teachings in four statements of elemental relationships. First, Jesus related faith and living, religion and ethics, belief and behavior. Second, his ethical teachings are related to the internal, not to the external; they are related to reality, not to regulation. Third, Jesus related his ethical activity to the Great Commandment of love of God. Fourth, he related his ethical teachings to his central teaching, that of the kingdom of God. These four statements merit explanation and expansion.

Faith and Living

First, Jesus related faith and living. This was basic to his own activity. You will remember that he began his ministry in the synagogue at Nazareth when he read from the book of Isaiah. This passage became the springboard and platform for Jesus' entire public ministry. Note the depth of social and ethical concern and the commitment to the needy expressed in the Isaiah passage—"to the poor. . . . to the captives . . . to the blind . . . those who are oppressed. . . ." (Luke 4:18; Isaiah 58:6, 61:1). Does this mean that Jesus' ministry was only horizontal, only concerned with those in physical, psychological, and social need? Not at all. These words express as much spiritual concern as they do social. They are related to faith as well as to living.

Faith "is born of obedience," said John Calvin. "The proof of Christianity really consists in 'following,'" declared Soren Kierkegaard. Karl Barth agreed: "Only the doer of the word is its real hearer." Jesus could see neither the need of people nor the concern of God as limited to one area of human existence. "The Spirit of the Lord is upon me, because he has anointed me. . . . He has sent me . . . to proclaim the acceptable year of the Lord" (Luke 4:18–19).

This intention is expressed in Jesus' teaching. One of the hardest statements that he ever uttered was in the Sermon on the Mount: "Love your enemies and pray for those who persecute you, so that you may be sons of your Father who is in heaven" (Matthew 5:44–45). In our day of "wars and rumors of wars" there is no more relevant concern than peace. Jesus makes the highest social demand upon us when he says, "Love your enemies and pray for those who persecute you." This demand is not simply a social and ethical one. The horizontal relationship with others is rooted in and required by the vertical relationship with God. The reason we should love our enemies and pray for them is "so that you may be sons of your Father who is in heaven" (Matthew 5:45). The demand for proper human relationship grows out of a relationship to God. The faith presented by Jesus cannot be divorced from his teaching and requirement upon our experience.

Those of us who claim to accept the ethics of Jesus and believe in his teachings must also accept the faith that he presented. If there is no belief in the God presented by Jesus Christ, there can be no understanding of the reason and motivation for Jesus' ethical teaching. The teaching becomes impossible idealism unless it is rooted in relationship with God. This vertical relationship is at the heart of Christian ethics. Any ethical system or activity that is not so related is less than Christian. Donald Shriver has rightly said, "You don't have to be a theologian to realize that Christian ethics and the ethics of Christians are often far apart."

This reality led Karl Barth to anchor his ethical teaching in the person and work of Jesus Christ. Bernard Ramm approved and commended the process to evangelicals:

> When the Christian church talks about moral issues in society apart from Jesus Christ, it impresses the populace as being prudish, moralistic, and isolated from the passions of the marketplace. Barth set a model for Evangelicals in his pastorate. He would not speak to

the labor or union groups without mentioning Jesus Christ, and he would not preach Jesus Christ in his church without commenting on social issues. By keeping ethics and Christology so close, Barth goes a long way toward preventing the church, in its ethical witness, as appearing only moralistic, only prudish, only interested in principles and not people.[5]

When Jesus makes one of his strongly idealistic demands upon us, it is not because it, necessarily, will work. We do not love our enemies because it is good political strategy. Remember that he loved his enemies even as they put him on a cross. He prayed for them. "Father, forgive them; for they know not what they do" (Luke 23:34). But his love was not effective in changing these people or in delivering him from death. Neither do we have a promise that love of our enemies will deliver us from pain or death. The reason for loving our enemies is not that it is effective or expedient politically, but because it is the will of God! Christians should be Christlike simply because that is the way God wants us to be. Jesus speaks of this utter commitment to God as basic to all of life.

Reality, Not Regulation

Second, Jesus related our ethical behavior to an internal, not an external, dimension. He is not interested in our ability or desire to live by rules and regulations. He is interested in our wholehearted commitment to the will of God—which may or may not be expressed in the form of a regulation. We ought to note that Jesus' ethical teaching is not distinctly different from that of the Old Testament. That is, what Jesus teaches about ethical behavior is not new and unique. Indeed, it is anticipated in Scripture. Moreover, many of the rabbis of his day and before had taught much of what Jesus taught. But he concentrated his teaching in a manner that was distinctive. He set aside the ceremonies and rules that were prescribed by rabbinic teachers. He demanded a thorough commitment to the will of God, an idea that had not been fully expressed by other teachers. Even so, Jesus had much in common with rabbinic teachers. Rabbinic Judaism was a religion of the law. At its best rabbinic Judaism was an explication of and a drawing of implications from the Torah. At its worst it reflected excessive casuistry.

But rabbinic teaching holds no monopoly in this arena. We face excessive legalism in our own day. Consider the following:

> When Marine Lance Corporal Candy Clark was beaten and raped by an officer in 1983, she reports that the officer was honorably discharged with full benefits. But when Marine Corps Captain John Moultak fell in love with Candy in 1984, and wanted to marry her the Corps gave him a court–martial and dishonorable discharge. Why? The court–martial Board at the Marine Corps Air Station in El Toro, California, ruled that Pilot Moultak's conduct in wanting to marry an enlisted woman, says *The New York Times,* was "conduct unbecoming an officer and a gentleman."[6]

The distinctive element of Jesus' ethical teaching was this internal flavor. His demand was upon reality, a commitment of spirit. When one obeyed the regulations without this sense of personal commitment to the will of God, Jesus was most disturbed. This religious hypocrisy was that which he spoke against most critically. Against religious leaders who were concerned with external detail more than with internal commitment to the will of God, he spoke a series of seven "woes" in Matthew 23. He repeatedly begins his comments with the statement, "Woe to you, scribes and Pharisees, hypocrites!" Today he would likely say that an ethical and moral life without a personal commitment to the will of God would be similarly meaningless. Woe to us if we live right externally but fail to relate to God at the depths of our existence!

Another way of saying this is that Jesus is more interested in our love than in our legalistic response to rules. Action that seeks only the appreciation of others—indeed, even action that is directed toward a currying of God's favor—is inadequate. Jesus' teaching, like that of the apostle Paul at a later date, indicated that ethical actions cannot make us acceptable to God. Rather, God loves us even in our sin, and we should live ethically out of responsive and responsible love to God.

The teaching that our ethical behavior should be a result of, rather than a means of, acceptance by God was an offense to many religious people of Jesus' day—as well as of our own. Today we assume that if we live a moral and ethical existence God will have to accept us. The thinking of the first century ran in the same vein.

In some ways, however, we are more legalistic and make greater demands upon ourselves than the legalists of the first century. We find Christian self-acceptance exceedingly difficult.

Keith Miller makes the point in a homey and humorous way:

> When I am unacceptable to myself, I often try to raise a furor of negative reactions and signals, evidently hoping that in the confusion no one will notice my weakness. You might call it the 'skunk' system. As everyone knows, when a skunk gets into trouble, he puts out a cloud of horrible odor that the other animals all know will stick to them if it gets on them. So every one else scrambles for cover, and when the 'smoke' clears, the skunk has walked to safety.
>
> Don't feel superior if you do not handle your vulnerability in this way. One of our little girls likes the 'turtle' method, which is simply to pull in her head and withdraw. After everyone tries to sniff around and bring her out, we all walk away, and she has arrived at a safe 'place' in which she can mope and feel sorry for herself in peace. Having checked with several people, it seems that this method is more popular than that of the skunk.[7]

We should help those in need, but not in order to impress people or to affect God. Recall Jesus' words about giving financial aid to the needy:

> "Thus, when you give alms, sound no trumpet before you, as the hypocrites do in the synagogues and in the streets, that they may be praised by men. Truly, I say to you, they have their reward. But when you give alms, do not let your left hand know what your right hand is doing, so that your alms may be in secret; and your Father who sees in secret will reward you" (Matthew 6:2–4).

Jesus does not mean here that we should not give to the needy. The point is that we should give out of a sense of love and devotion to God. We should not seek the praise of others through such giving, nor should we expect the act of giving to gain the favor of God. In other words, this action, and all other social actions, should grow out of a love for God, not out of an imagined divine demand. In short, we are to love because we have been loved. We are not to love in order that we may be loved.

The Great Commandment Ethic

Third, Jesus related service to humanity with what has been

called the "Great Commandment." Love is central in this commandment—love for both God and others: " '. . . you shall love the Lord your God with all your heart, and with all your soul, and with all your mind, and with all your strength' " (Mark 12:30).

Pudd'nhead Wilson says, "By trying we can easily learn to endure adversity. Another man's, I mean."[8] In our day we manifest less than a Christian spirit in viewing the adversities of the poor. Indeed, some criticize them as taking advantage of the government's welfare system. But Peter Devries maintains, "We are not on this earth to see through one another, but to see one another through." If the world cannot accept this philosophy, the Christian must. The poor were the objects of our Lord's concern and action, not his advice. Oscar Wilde has well said, "To recommend thrift to the poor is both grotesque and insulting. It is advising a man who is starving to eat less."

We should recognize that the Christian church has brought great healing to the world through its service to humanity in relief and development projects. The following illustration from the Second World War can be multiplied hundreds of times:

> The citizens of one small and relatively poor county in Indiana have recently sent one thousand pounds of dried milk to the people of Austria. Those who made possible this considerable gift have never, so far as they know, seen any of the recipients. Most of the residents of the little Indiana county are Protestants whereas nearly all the recipients are Roman Catholics. The whole endeavor was the result of the dedicated effort of the members of two or three little churches.[9]

Love for God demands a love for others. Love for others, in turn, demands service to them. The service motif is not only reflected in Jesus' ministry, but it is woven throughout all of his teaching. Consider the story of the good Samaritan. The man who brought the story forth from Jesus was endeavoring to involve our Lord in a theological argument. Jesus refused the argument. After telling the story of one who was concerned for a man in need and of his efforts in meeting that need Jesus turned the question back to his tempter. The proper question is not who, hypothetically, *is* my neighbor, but who really *acts* the part of neighbor. Henry Wadsworth Longfellow said that the only way to have a friend is to be one.

Obviously the one who cares and serves acts the part of a neighbor and therefore *is* a neighbor—regardless of geographical proximity or racial similarity. Jesus refused to argue about theology at this point. He only gave a command: "Go and do likewise" (Luke 10:37).

Love toward others and the desire to serve them was most clearly reflected in Jesus' activity on his last night on earth. None of the disciples had taken the servant's task of washing the feet of his friends. Their feet were dusty from the paths of Palestine. Jesus disrobed himself, tied a towel around his waist, filled a basin with water and proceeded to wash their feet. Would you like to know what God is like? That is what God is like! Would you like to know what love does? That was love in action. If we love people, we will serve them. Jesus indicates that if we love God, we will serve those in need.

Thus, the Christian faith demands such action from us. So wrote Professor J. S. Whale:

> Faith without ethical consequences is a lie. Good works must necessarily follow faith. God does not need our sacrifices but he, nevertheless, appointed a representative to receive them, namely our neighbor. The neighbor always represents the invisible Christ.[10]

The Kingdom of God

Finally, Jesus relates the ethical demand to his central teaching, that of the kingdom of God. If God rules effectively within our experience, Jesus taught, we shall reflect God's love. God's sovereignty is not something that is waiting for the distant future. Jesus taught that the kingdom of God was in the midst of the people to whom he came.

We might feel that the kingdom of God is entirely in the future. The ideal day when God is manifestly in control of the affairs of this world is far from us, it seems. We recognize the reality of human sin and the complexities of the social structures in which we are involved today. Nevertheless, Jesus' life and teaching inaugurated the kingdom.

Jesus was not only idealistic in his demands and understanding of God's will. He was also realistic concerning our self-centeredness. Still, he would never scale down the demands of God's rule to our present level of existence. His teaching always concerned the ideal will of God. Jesus would not compromise in order to enable everyone and anyone to meet his demands. If God really rules, and if we are truly God's servants, we shall not modify God's will.

Note the words Jesus used to exemplify this high calling: "No one can serve two masters; for either he will hate the one and love the other, or he will be devoted to the one and despise the other. You cannot serve God and mammon" (Matthew 6:24). There can be no compromise with the ultimate ideal. Hear him again:

> "Do not resist one who is evil. But if any one strikes you on the right cheek, turn to him the other also; and if any one would sue you and take your coat, let him have your cloak as well; and if any one forces you to go one mile, go with him two miles. Give to him who begs from you, and do not refuse him who would borrow from you" (Matthew 5:39–42).

Imagine what would happen to our entire society if we really tried to practice this kind of thing! Sadly, we are awed by these standards and begin immediately to scale down the thrust of Jesus' teaching when we read these words. Yet he refused to scale down what God ultimately wanted of us. If God is really our Guide, we should obey God's will. Will obedience to God change our enemies into our friends? Jesus gives no implication that this is the case. We should follow divine guidelines simply because God desires us to do so. Hear Jesus again:

> "Love your enemies and pray for those who persecute you, so that you may be sons of your Father who is in heaven; for he makes his sun rise on the evil and on the good, and sends rain on the just and on the unjust. For if you love those who love you, what reward have you? Do not even the tax collectors do the same? And if you salute only your brethren, what more are you doing than others? Do not even the Gentiles do the same? You, therefore, must be perfect, as your heavenly Father is perfect" (Matthew 5:44–48).

So the standard that Jesus holds out is perfection—the perfection of God the Creator!

Jesus tells us that we should be concerned about others. What becomes intensely clear is that *I am* my brother's and sister's keeper. If I refuse to recognize the claims of my brother or sister on my existence; if I refuse to aid them in their need; if I pass by on the other side unconcerned, I am behaving contrary to the will of God.

Biblical scholars and theologians have endeavored to fit this high teaching of Jesus into the practical situations of our complex society. Some have felt that Jesus' demands can only be met in the coming kingdom of God. Others have felt that the teachings are wonderful ideals, but that our self–centeredness makes it impossible for us to live up to them. Still others have suggested that the teaching of Jesus does not translate into rules for everyday living.

There is probably some truth in each of these suggestions. We cannot expect to live perfect lives. Nevertheless, this inability does not negate Jesus' demands. We should seek to do the will of God even when it exceeds our grasp. Jesus calls us to radical discipleship.

In conclusion, note that Jesus walked this road himself. Indeed, he promises to walk with us in our day. Jesus is not only the perfect expression of what God is like. He is also our Savior. He comes bringing the ideal demands of God to our experience. He also comes bringing the power of God into the humblest of human hearts. The life of discipleship is not a way of attainment through struggle and striving. On the contrary, it is a way of responding to the divine love that has grasped us in Jesus Christ. "We love, because he first loved us" (1 John 4:19). And because we love God, we love both sister and brother.

Chapter Twelve

Did You Hear the Story?

The Teachings of Jesus through Parables

To be a good conversationalist is something of an art. Many of us have to work at it extensively. There is one time, however, when everyone seems to get into the act. That is when stories are told. Have you found yourself hearing a story that reminded you of another? When you tell it you remember another. Then another person remembers a story—and so it goes. One story leads to another. They involve us.

We rarely feel ourselves to be so needed and appreciated as when we are telling a story to a wide-eyed child. We feel that we are contributing something of ourselves to a growing life. There is a complete openness, an absorption of young life in everything that is being said.

Stories in speeches and sermons also make an impression. Years after the idea or argument has been forgotten, the story remains. Imagine the frustration of the minister who tells a story to illustrate a particular point in a sermon and finds it is the story and not the point that is remembered! The story was intended to be a servant, but the servant became greater than the master.

But all is not lost. This analysis simply underscores the value of the story. Insights can be communicated by storytelling that cannot be passed along in any other form.

The story is as old as the human race. Before we had classrooms, chalkboards, computers, teaching machines, or even teachers, the story was told. Our ancient ancestors gathered around the campfire in the evening, and told the stories of the great heroes and heroines of the past. These were passed along to the hearers' children and to their children's children. Such stories were told with more than a view to entertain. They communicated some of the heritage of the community. They were tools of transmission for an entire culture.

Long before Jesus came with his well-known stories, storytelling was a popular device used among the people of God. Probably the most famous telling of a story in the Old Testament is the one Nathan the prophet told to David the king. Nathan told the king a story, but he had no intention of entertaining. He had a point to make, and it could be made effectively only through this avenue.

David the king wanted the wife of Uriah. Uriah was one of his soldiers; David arranged his death. As a result he was able to have the desired Bathsheba as his wife (2 Samuel 11). It seems that David assumed his right to take the life of Uriah. There is no evidence that David had a guilty conscience. Presumably he thought that, as king, he could deal with his people as he wished.

Nathan the prophet could not condone this wrong. He approached the king and told him this story:

> There were two men in a certain city, the one rich and the other poor. The rich man had very many flocks and herds; but the poor man had nothing but one little ewe lamb, which he had bought. And he brought it up, and it grew up with him and with his children; it used to eat of his morsel, and drink from his cup, and lie in his bosom, and it was like a daughter to him. Now there came a traveler to the rich man, and he was unwilling to take one of his own flock or herd to prepare for the wayfarer who had come to him, but he took the poor man's lamb, and prepared it for the man who had come to him (2 Samuel 12:1-4).

David was a large-hearted man, and reacted violently against the wealthy man in the story. Perhaps he sensed his own wrong unconsciously, and projected this wrong upon the selfishness of the wealthy man. In any event, his anger was kindled and he said to Nathan, "As the Lord lives, the man who has done this thing deserves to die; and he shall restore the lamb fourfold, because he did this thing, and because he had no pity" (2 Samuel 12:5, 6).

Before David knew what had actually happened, he was forced to face the enormity of his guilt. Nathan's words struck home, "You are the man" (2 Samuel 12:7). The prophet continued by interpreting the story and applying it to the wrongdoing of his king. David repented. The traditional expression of his penitence is reflected in the fifty–first psalm:

> Create in me a clean heart, O God, and put a new and right spirit within me. Cast me not away from thy presence, and take not thy holy Spirit from me. Restore to me the joy of thy salvation, and uphold me with a willing spirit. Then will I teach transgressors thy ways, and sinners will return to thee (Psalm 51:10–13).

Storytelling is not limited to the Scriptures. Across the centuries Jewish rabbis have used stories to put their messages across. Consider the story of the Fox and the Fishes which is reputed to have come from the mouth of Rabbi Akiba, a leading Palestinian leader of the second century:

> Once the evil kingship ordered the Israelites not to busy themselves with the Law. Pappus ben Jehudah met Rabbi Akiba holding an assembly in the street and busying himself with the Law. He said to him, "Akiba, do you not fear the evil kingship?" Akiba replied, "I will tell you a parable. What is the matter like? It is like a fox who went along a river bank and saw fishes which gathered together from one place to another. The fox said to them: 'Why do you flee away?' They replied, 'Because of the nets which men cast over us.' He said to them, 'If you were minded to mount up on dry land, we might dwell, you and I, as my fathers dwelt with your fathers.' They said to him, 'Are you he of whom it is said that he is the cleverest of beasts? You are not clever but only rather foolish. If we are already afraid in the place of our life (i.e., in the water), how much more would we be in the place of our death (i.e., on dry land)!' So with us too. If we fear now where we sit and busy ourselves with the Law, in which it is written, 'For that is thy life and the length of thy days' (Deut. 30:20), how much more so if we go off and neglect it!"[1]

Neither the story told by Nathan nor the story told by Rabbi Akiba was given simply to entertain. Nathan told his story to awaken the conscience of the king. Akiba told his story to encourage a fear of God and study of the Law.

It is well known that Jesus used storytelling in his teaching. This technique rose to its height in his masterful hands. One third of his recorded teaching is in the form of stories.

From the Known to the Unknown

The stories of Jesus are called parables. Definitions of the "parable" are many. It has been called a "simple story with a spiritual meaning," or "an earthly story with a heavenly meaning." And it is this. It begins on the simple or earthly level that we already know. From here, the parable moves to a spiritual or heavenly message. It is basic to any good teaching method, of course, to move from the known to the unknown. Teachers begin at the point of the student's knowledge and move to that which has not yet been appropriated or appreciated. Thus Jesus would commonly begin his parables with the words, "The kingdom of heaven is like. . . ."

The hallmarks of Jesus' parables were clarity and simplicity. His primary audience was the common people. Abraham Lincoln once said to Chauncey Depew,

> They say I tell a great many stories; I reckon I do, but I have found in the course of a long experience that common people, take them as they run, are more easily informed through the medium of a broad illustration than in any other way, and as to what the hypercritical few may think, I don't care.

Addressing common people is the particular responsibility of the preacher of the gospel. One of the great preachers in America is Dr. Thomas W. Gillespie, president of Princeton Theological Seminary. He was inaugurated to this position on September 1, 1983. On that occasion he began his inaugural address with a confession:

> The last time I stood in this pulpit, I was preaching my middler sermon here at the Seminary. . . . The result was accurately stated in the critique which followed. Professor MacLeod said to me: 'Mr. Gillespie, if your name were not on this manuscript, I would have sworn that it had been written by George Adam Smith and preached to Queen Victoria. Mr. Gillespie, come down from your theological high horse and preach to Aunt Fannie in the front pew.'[2]

Too often the preacher is neither communicating in simple

words, nor to needy, common people. This fact led Edna St. Vincent Millay to write "To Jesus on His Birthday:"

> For this your mother sweated in the cold,
> For this you bled upon the bitter tree:
> A yard of tinsel ribbon bought and sold;
> A paper wreath, a day at home for me.
> The merry bells ring out, the people kneel;
> Up goes the man of God before the crowd;
> With voice of honey and with eyes of steel
> He drones your humble gospel to the proud.
> Nobody listens. Less than the wind that blows
> Are all your words to us you died to save.
> O Prince of Peace! O Sharon's dewy Rose!
> How mute you lie within your vaulted grave
> The stone the angel rolled away with tears.[3]

Ron Reid has communicated parabolically (though without using a parable) in *Sports Illustrated*:

Soon after his first child was born, Yogi Berra called fellow baseball player Jimmy Piersall, who has nine children, and asked for a few tips on changing diapers. "Yogi," explained Piersall, "you take a diaper and put it in the shape of a baseball diamond, with you at bat. Then fold second base down to home. Take the baby's bottom and put it in the pitcher's mound. Then pin first base and third to home plate." "That's easy," said Berra. "I can do that." "Wait a minute, Yogi," cautioned Piersall. "One thing about this game—when it starts to rain, there's no postponement."[4]

The word "parable" is interesting in derivation. The first four letters mean "alongside" in Greek. The last three letters reflect our word "to throw." Derivatively then, the word "parable" means a thing "thrown alongside." That is, the parable is a story that is thrown alongside the truth it is meant to communicate.

A parable does not speak literally, but is placed alongside that which it actually intends. The natural world and daily experience point to the spiritual—God's rule and sovereignty. Dean Inge said, "Almost all teaching consists in comparing the unknown with the known, the strange with the familiar."

The story or parable method carries the value of reality and concreteness. It brings us out of the realm of the speculative and the abstract. It deals with real flesh and blood, deep feelings, desires, dreams, and hostilities. Oliver Cromwell once addressed his followers and said, "We speak things." His emphasis, of course, was upon the concrete and actual. Speaking "things" delivers us from the vagaries of speculation. The story form relates us to real life.

Contemporary preachers are indebted to Professor Ernest Best for his excellent guide to biblical preaching. He shares a story that relates our Lord's life to our life today:

> The chaplain of a boys' school once gave a talk to his students which he illustrated by showing them a hammer, a saw, and other tools. Afterwards he met one of the mothers, and she said to him, "Jimmy came home and told us about your talk and now he realizes that Jesus was a real man." The next day he met another of the mothers and she said, "Billy came home and told us about your talk. Why don't you stick to the Bible and teach the boys what's in it?"[5]

Professor Helmut Thielicke has served as probably the outstanding scholar–preacher of the past generation. He conversed with academicians in his post as professor of theology and provost of the University of Hamburg. He made the faith understandable to the masses through his regular preaching to an overflow congregation. He understood well the importance of relating the gospel to the life of his hearers.

For example, he delighted in describing a group of primitive bushmen from southern Africa who were taken to a great technological exhibition. They were transported by air. They were shown computers and electronic brains. Scientists speculated as to what would impress these people the most. To their surprise it was an ordinary kitchen faucet. The jet flight and the technological magic were from fairy tales, from gods and demons. But the faucet with immediate water related to their every day needs. The foreign became familiar and real at this point of need.

Stories can grow out of our experience. They need not—indeed, should not—be pulled from the literary masterpieces. The point of the story as a teaching medium is not that it will be impressive in itself. It is rather that it will guide us to that which it is trying to express.

Jesus' stories and parables related to things that we can see and feel. This is important in our learning. We should see something in a parable. The point should be obvious. Moreover, we should feel it. When you hear a story that captures your imagination and affects your emotions, you simply cannot go to sleep. You are still involved. Jesus' stories were of this nature.

What are the keys to the interpretation of Jesus' stories? What was it that he was actually trying to teach? We might note that there were as many different teachings as there were parables. Certainly each story had its own particular point and emphasis. Indeed, the most important thing to note is that parables have one primary emphasis. They are given to make one point clear.

We should not try to identify every detail in a parable. A parable is not an allegory.

The classical and well-known failure to see this point is in the ancient interpretation of the parable of the good Samaritan presented by St. Augustine. Consider Luke's account:

> And Jesus answering said, A certain *man* went down from Jerusalem to Jericho, and fell among thieves, which stripped him of his raiment, and wounded *him*, and departed, leaving *him* half dead. And by chance there came down a certain priest that way; and when he saw him, he passed by on the other side. And likewise a Levite, when he was at the place, came and looked *on him,* and passed by on the other side. But a certain Samaritan, as he journeyed, came where he was; and when he saw him, he had compassion *on him.* And went to *him,* and bound up his wounds, pouring in oil and wine, and set him on his own beast, and brought him to an inn, and took care of him. And on the morrow when he departed, he took out two pence, and gave *them* to the host, and said unto him, Take care of him; and whatsoever thou spendest more, when I come again, I will repay thee. Which now of these three, thinkest thou, was neighbour unto him that fell among the thieves? And he said, He that shewed mercy on him. Then said Jesus unto him, Go and do thou likewise (Luke 10:30–37 KJV).

Augustine tried to interpret this parable as an allegory—seeing many points of interpretation. He tells us that the man who went down from Jerusalem to Jericho was Adam, our forefather. Jerusalem was considered the heavenly city of blessing from which Adam fell. Jericho meant the moon, Augustine said. This is because the moon comes into being; it becomes large and then small, and finally disappears. The thieves are the devil and his angels. They stripped Adam of his immortality. They beat him and robbed him, and thus persuaded him to sin. They left him half dead, Augustine said, because a person can know something about God even in a sinful condition. (Thus, the man was "half dead.") The priest and the Levite represent the priesthood and values of the Old Testament that were not useful for salvation. The Samaritan was the Lord Jesus Christ. The binding of the wounds was the holding back of sin. The oil is comfort and hope. The wine is the exhortation to work fervently. The beast is Jesus' body; the setting of the man on the beast illustrated the belief in Christ's incarnation. The inn to which the good Samaritan came is the church where we are refreshed on our way to the heavenly country. The next day, when the Samaritan left the inn, stands for the time following Jesus' resurrection. The two pennies are the two demands of love or the promise of this life and of future life or even the two sacraments of baptism and the Lord's Supper. The innkeeper is the apostle Paul. The promise to pay any further expenses by the Samaritan predicts Paul's refraining from marriage or his working for a living with his own hands.[6]

It is obvious that this interpretation is not what Jesus meant! Augustine was allegorizing to an extreme. Rather, Jesus put across a single point—what it is to *act* as a neighbor. It is the person who is concerned, who cares, that is the neighbor. To draw more than this conclusion from the story is to miss the main point.

The Purpose of the Parables

What was the purpose of the parables in Jesus' ministry? Why did he use the story form so often? In the first place, as we have noted, the story helps us to understand. It is like the illustration that a minister uses in a sermon. It begins at a level that we recognize and carries us on to what may not be so obvious.

When Martin Luther King, Jr., received the Nobel Peace prize, his father sat nearby as Martin gave his acceptance speech. As always, "Daddy King" encouraged his son with the words, "Make it plain, son!"

Verbosity, circumlocution, and obscure language too often substitute for clear, simple communication. For example: "There is an ongoing viability to the aggregate of human enterprises that attain a terminal configuration without being adversely impacted." Or, as Shakespeare said more directly: "All's well that ends well."

Dr. Frank E. Gaebelein tells of a conversation with the late C.S. Lewis at Magdalene College, Oxford, in 1953:

> While we were discussing the need for clarity in writing and speaking, Dr. Lewis told me about hearing a young parson preach. Very much in earnest, the young man ended his sermon like this, "And now, my friends, if you do not believe these truths, there may be for you grave eschatological consequences." "I went to him afterwards," said Dr. Lewis and asked, "Did you mean that they would be in danger of hell?" "Why, yes," the parson said. "Then why in the world didn't you say so?" Lewis replied.

Karl Barth was, likely, the most prolific theological scholar of the twentieth century. Asked by an American audience to summarize the gist of his enormous books on theology, Barth charmed them by quoting from a Sunday school song:

> Jesus loves me,
> This I know,
> For the Bible
> Tells me so.

Barth could so speak with integrity, inasmuch as he had done his theological homework carefully. We should emulate both his care in study and his clarity in expression. Simplicity that is not born of such study is inadequate and often misleading.

Nils Bohr has said, "The opposite of truth is not falsehood but simplification."

We should note also that some stories are told in order to make us think. This is notably true of Jesus' parables. Sometimes he would present a story in order to puzzle us just a bit. When we begin to think about the story further the meaning comes through. The process of forcing us to think is as great in value as is the knowledge that is gained.

In addition, there seems to be a purpose in Jesus' parables that is not particularly acceptable to us. There is at least one occasion in which he seems to indicate that the parables were *not* given for the purpose of understanding.

When Alaska governor Jay Hammond visited China in 1979, he met with Vice Premier Deng Xiaoping. The meeting was televised for both Chinese and American audiences. Deng asked Hammond through an interpreter what he thought of the Chinese system of government. "What was I supposed to say to that—especially with people back home watching?" Hammond mused. "Finally I said, 'Any regime that manages to do away with the necktie can't be all bad.' " There was an exchange between Deng and the interpreter, who then turned to Hammond, with no expression at all and said, "The vice premier says you crack him up!" There are times when an indirect answer is best.

Jesus spoke clearly and directly. He did not mince words. On those rare occasions when he spoke obliquely, it was with a purpose. Unlike Governor Hammond, he sought no diplomatic way of saying the expedient and acceptable thing. Even so, Jesus' meaning is not always clear at first glance. On occasion, Jesus' parables seemed to have been given in order to keep us from understanding:

> And when he was alone, those who were about him with the twelve asked him concerning the parables. And he said to them, "To you has been given the secret of the kingdom of God, but for those outside everything is in parables; so that they may indeed see but not perceive, and may indeed hear but not understand; lest they should turn again, and be forgiven" (Mark 4:10–12).

At first glance, this statement leads us to think that Jesus told parables to people who were not his followers in order to confuse them. His teachings were cast in story form, it seems, so that people might not understand and thus, not be forgiven. This analysis constitutes a serious problem. It seems so utterly contrary to the whole thrust of Jesus' activities and attitudes throughout his ministry.

In struggling with this issue, we should bear in mind that Jesus told stories so that we might bring something of our own perceptions and understandings to his words as well as draw from them the teaching that he was communicating. Consider a modern communication:

> "Captain, there's a personal message to you from the admiral," reported the communications officer.

"Well, read it to me."

The officer read: "Of all the blundering, stupid, dimwitted idiots, you take the cake."

"Have that decoded at once!" demanded the captain.

Professor Thomas C. Oden has studied extensively the use of parables by Soren Kierkegaard:

> The parables clearly fall into Kierkegaard's category of indirect communication, because they confront us with a *choice* between the possibilities of self–understanding, so that in the process of having to choose, we discover ourselves, or something of ourselves. . . . That this task of indirect communication is exceedingly difficult is recognized by Kierkegaard in this analogy: "To stop a man on the street and stand still while talking to him, is not so difficult as to say something to a passer–by in passing, without standing still and without delaying the other, without attempting to persuade him to go the same way, but giving him instead an impulse to go precisely his own way. Such is the relation between one existing individual and another when the communication concerns the truth as existential inwardness."[7]

We should remember further that Jesus did not speak in the Greek in which Mark wrote; he spoke the common language of the Jewish people of his day, Aramaic. The Aramaic statement that he used could have been translated into Greek either with the word "who" or "lest." Our authorized translation indicates that the translation should be "lest," so that Jesus' teachings come in parables to those outside *lest* they see and understand. It is probable, however, that Jesus originally said that his parables came to those who were outside *who* saw but did not understand. Thus Jesus is not talking about the purpose of his speaking in parables but the factual result that eventuated from his speaking in parables. He spoke in parables to his followers who understood, but those who were not his followers did not understand. This, incidentally, is true not only of Jesus' stories, but of all of his teaching.

Although Jesus presented dozens of parables, there are but four main thrusts in Jesus' teaching in these parables. First is that the rule and relationships of God have begun in our midst. Second, we see the kind of people we should be within this relationship with God. Third, there is a great judgment to come, and we should be prepared for it. Fourth, and most important, God loves us deeply. The final point was the central emphasis of Jesus' teachings. It also spoke to the greatest need of the people both of Jesus' day and of ours. Malcolm Muggeridge is representative of the people of modernity. The sophisticated, and often cynical, editor of *Punch* was converted late in life. In *Jesus Rediscovered*, he witnesses to the power of Jesus' teachings as reflected in the Gospels:

> Is it not extraordinary to the point of being a miracle, that so loose and ill-constructed a narrative in an antique translation of a dubious text should after so many centuries still have the power to quell and dominate a restless, opinionated, over-exercised and under-nourished twentieth-century mind?[8]

God's gracious love is reflected in three stories in Luke 15. The stories describe a lost sheep, a lost coin, and a lost boy. In these stories the essence of the gospel is clearly explicated. God loves us beyond our deserving, even though we are foolish and self-centered. In our confusion we wander far from our relationship with God. We even become estranged from ourselves. We wonder if we can ever be accepted. Then we are amazed to find that we are always loved. God is concerned for us, and brings us home.

The reconciliation is not our doing. God seeks us out and receives us in love. What is God like? Not a judge who condemns. Not a bookkeeper who records our wrongs for judgment. Rather, God is a loving Father who waits, who seeks, and who casts aside all propriety in rushing to receive us with open arms. This love speaks to our need. We are all like the boy who has gone far from home. When we come to ourselves, however, we can return to find that the Father is waiting, watching, seeking. God loves us and is concerned for us. When we return we find that we are accepted, and we are home.

Chapter Thirteen

Is There Life after Death?

The Teachings of Jesus Concerning the Afterlife

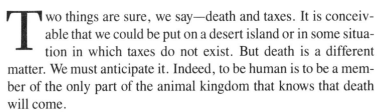

Two things are sure, we say—death and taxes. It is conceivable that we could be put on a desert island or in some situation in which taxes do not exist. But death is a different matter. We must anticipate it. Indeed, to be human is to be a member of the only part of the animal kingdom that knows that death will come.

Death stands over us like a ghostly specter. We do our best with euphemisms. We speak of the one who has departed, passed on, gone to eternal reward, or gained rest; there are a dozen other nice ways of avoiding the simple statement that someone died. Moreover, our cemeteries are some of the most lovely places in the community. The beautiful landscaping and the perennial sense of spring take visitors away from the thought of death.

Even so, most would agree with W. Somerset Maugham's advice: "Death is a very dull, dreary affair, and my advice to you is to have nothing whatsoever to do with it."

This sentiment is understandable. Death is not attractive. Indeed, the Bible calls death "the last great enemy." We try hard to ignore it. We would like to escape it. But death still awaits us. All of our efforts can't get us around it.

We should, rather, look beyond death. Consider the helpful

insights of Christian psychiatrist Paul Tournier:

> My old age has meaning. I can live through it with my gaze still fixed
> before me, and not behind me, because I am on my way to a destina-
> tion beyond death. There is no need for great sermons to help people
> to grasp that. Durkheim tells of a visit he made to the bedside of an
> old friend on the point of death. The friend talked to him at great
> length, as if to delude himself, of a project which he certainly could
> not carry out. 'You would do better,' Durkheim said to him simply,
> 'to fix your eyes beyond death.' There was a long silence. Then his
> friend said, quietly, the two words, 'Thank you!'[1]

This story leads to the question: After death . . . then what? Will
death be the end? Are we composed of just so many physical elements? Is the real personality or soul only a combination of chemi-
cals within a physical frame? When the lungs cease expanding and
the heart stops beating, is that the end?—Not for the believer.
Robert A. Millikan, one of America's great physicists, said, "We
have come from somewhere and we are going somewhere. The
great architect of the universe never built a stairway that leads to
nowhere."

Benjamin Franklin was buried in the yard of Christ Church in his
beloved Philadelphia. Interestingly, the simple flat stone over his
grave does not contain the epitaph that Franklin himself composed
for such a monument:

> Like the cover of an old book,
>   Its contents torn out;
> And stripped of its lettering and gilding,
>   Lies here food for worms.
> But the work shall not be lost
>   For it will—as he believes—appear once more
> In a new and more elegant edition
>   Revised and corrected by the Author.

When Charles Haddon Spurgeon approached death's dark door,
he exclaimed, "Now the great adventure!" Dwight L. Moody sang
out, "This is my coronation!" Who can forget the final words of
the U. S. Senate Chaplain Peter Marshall? If you saw the film, "A
Man Called Peter," you will remember that Peter was being
wheeled to an ambulance following his mortal heart attack. To his

beloved Catherine, he said, "I'll see you in the morning!"

A minister of the last generation dreamed up a little story that may help us in our thinking about life beyond death. It is in the form of a dialogue between two unborn babies who are in their mother's womb. They have been given the ability to talk, and they engage in conversation after being in the womb for several months. The one baby is an unbeliever. He says, "We shall be dying in a matter of days. We shall be going out of this world where we have spent our lives these many months. This will be the end. There has been no ultimate purpose in our living here. Now we move out of this dark world and face death. This will be the end of everything. We are without hope." But the other unborn child is a believer. She says, "I cannot agree that this is the end. I believe that there is a God who has made us for this life and another to come. We have been made to see things that have never been ours to experience. We have been made to enter upon the fuller life. This life has been without meaning unless there is more. I am confident that this life is merely a preparation for a larger and better life beyond. I believe that what you are calling death may actually be our birth. It will not be the end but the beginning of our fuller life."

Dorothy Gilman similarly reflected on life after life in *A New Kind of Country:*

> Euripides said, "Who knows but life be that which men call death, and death what men call life?"
>
> I like this. I picture myself about to die. I don't want to leave, but my time is up, my span completed. I say good–bye, clinging a little to those people I've loved and enjoyed. I fill my eyes for a last time with the incredible colors and beauty around me and, as I brace myself and begin the struggle of letting go, I feel the darkness sweep over me. I'm precipitated through a long, dark tunnel into a bright light that blinds me. Hands roughly handle me. I cry out in protest and hear a voice exclaim, "It's a girl, Mrs. G! You've just given birth to a healthy baby girl." And I have entered what we call life.[2]

Any thought of life after death was fed by two tributaries in Jesus' day. On the one hand, there was the thought of the Greek world as it followed Plato, the renowned philosopher. The Greeks assumed the immortality of the soul. The human soul was made for eternity, but during human life this soul was imprisoned within the body. Thus the body was something of a cage that must be destroyed at death in order that the soul might be released. On the other hand, the Jewish world reflected the thinking of the Old Testament. Implicit in the Old Testament Scriptures was the idea of the resurrection of the body rather than the immortality of the soul. Note that this idea was only implicit; it became more clearly understood within the pages of the New Testament.

The idea of the life to come, combined with the living presence of Jesus Christ, was the primary motivating force in the early Christian church. The early Christians cared for widows and orphans. They collected abandoned babies outside of the walls of Rome and gave them homes. Out of their poverty, the Christians shared with the poor. These believers, who looked toward the age to come, were most involved in the needs of the present age. Following their footsteps, English Evangelicals and American Christians led in the abolition of slavery. With their citizenship in heaven they were the best of the citizens of earth. Conversely, ineffectiveness in this world is marked by a lack of concern for the world to come. Someone has said: "Aim at heaven and you will get earth 'thrown in': aim at earth and you will get neither."

Probably the most important Old Testament passage related to the concept of life after death is in Daniel 12:2. It reads: "And many of those who sleep in the dust of the earth shall awake, some to everlasting life, and some to shame and everlasting contempt." Inasmuch as this passage speaks of those "who sleep in the dust of the earth" and who "shall awake," it implies resurrection. The Old Testament does not assume that persons are immortal souls locked within the prison houses of bodies. On the contrary, the Old Testament sees human beings as a combination of body and soul. Neither really exists without the other. Inasmuch as we are this body–soul combination, rising to everlasting life or everlasting contempt is a resurrection as whole beings.

Throughout the Bible the body is understood to be more than a physical unit. A better understanding of body—as implied in the Old Testament and made explicit within the New Testament— would be the word "personality." Biblically speaking, the word "body" would be better understood as a frame or as an organism. The body in this sense is the whole being, that is, an individual personality.

This definition speaks squarely to our Christian understanding of the resurrection of the body. The resurrection of the body in the Bible is not meant to be simple resuscitation of a physical body. It is more than a bringing back of human breath or of renewing the beating of the human heart. It is, rather, a bringing of a new and deathless life into the human organism. The life that grows out of resurrection is a far greater life than that which could be known before physical death. Spirituals emphasize resurrection as "the great gettin' up morning."

Pharisees vs. Sadducees

We now should turn to another pair of viewpoints that constituted background for Jesus' teaching about life after death. These views are best expressed by the two notable sectarian groups within Judaism, the Pharisees and the Sadducees.

The differing views of Pharisees and Sadducees concerning life after death are expressed clearly in the Acts of the Apostles of Paul before the council in Jerusalem. Luke tells us that Paul perceived one part of the council to be composed of Sadducees and the other of Pharisees. Thus he went to the heart of the accusation. He reminded them that he had been reared as a Pharisee. He further suggested that he was being tried because of his hope in the resurrection of the dead. Of course, we know that he was there because of his conviction that Jesus Christ had been raised from the dead. As soon as Paul brought in an understanding of the resurrection as the reason for his indictment, he divided the council. Why?— Because of the distinction of viewpoints between the Pharisees and the Sadducees on the resurrection of the dead.

The Sadducees were the ruling priests and leaders in Jesus' and Paul's day. They controlled the high priesthood and the leading offices of temple activity. They believed that God was rather distant. The Eternal, in their view, was not intimately concerned with or denied the resurrection of the dead. The Sadducees only held to the first five books of the Hebrew Bible as being sacred Scripture, and these books, they felt, did not teach the resurrection.

The Pharisees, on the other hand, were the popular religious party. They were more pious than the Sadducees. Their religious outlook impressed the people more than did that of the more politically-oriented Sadducees. The Pharisees believed that God was intimately related with human life and was active within it. They believed in the resurrection of the dead. Finally, the Pharisees looked forward to a coming life for those who obeyed the rabbinic teachings and delighted in the law of God.

So how did Jesus' teachings relate to this disagreement? The Sadducees rightly sensed that Jesus believed in life after death, as did the Pharisees. They presented him with an argument that they hoped would be impossible for him to handle and would thus embarrass him. It is likely that they had used this same argument at various times on their Pharisaic friends. Their argument was drawn from the law of Moses. It related to a practice called levirate marriage. This term referred to the duty of a man to marry the widow of his deceased brother in the event that his brother had no sons. If a man left no sons, his name would perish from the earth. Thus, a practice had been developed whereby the dead man's oldest brother would take the widow as his own wife until she had a male child. This male child was naturally the son of the living man, but officially the son of the deceased. Thus the name of the deceased was continued.

The Sadducees formulated an account in which seven different brothers had died and each of the six had taken the widow of his previously deceased brother—all without success in bringing forth sons. The problem the Sadducees presented was in this final question: "In the resurrection whose wife will she be?" (Mark 12:23).

Jesus pointed out their error in two directions—in neither understanding the Scriptures nor the power of God. They did not understand their own Scriptures—even the first five books of the Old Testament—inasmuch as they did not see that God was the God of the living in these books. He referred them to the time when Moses heard the voice of God from the burning bush. God said, "I am the God of your father, the God of Abraham, the God of Isaac, and the God of Jacob" (Exodus 3:6). Jesus went on to point out that God was the God of living patriarchs, not of corpses. Inasmuch as God said, "I *am* the God of" these men (author's emphasis), they must in turn be alive. God did not say, "I *was* the God of" these men.

Jesus also suggested that the Sadducees did not understand the power of God. God could make a situation in eternity where present human relationships are not necessary. He went on to suggest that in heaven there would be neither marrying nor giving in marriage. That is, there would not be a limitation to present relationships. Clearly, Jesus disagreed with the Sadducees. He took a firm stand in a belief in life after death and of the resurrection of the dead.

Billy Graham had the opportunity to speak with the venerable postwar chancellor of West Germany, Konrad Adenauer. After exchanging greetings and pouring a cup of coffee for Graham, Adenauer turned to him and said, "Young man, do you believe that Jesus Christ is alive?" Graham replied, "Yes, sir, I do!" Adenauer said, "So do I. If Jesus Christ is not alive, then I see no hope for the world. It is the fact of the resurrection that gives me hope for the future." And as the aged chancellor spoke those words his eyes lighted up.

Henry VanDyke, American preacher, poet and philosopher, expressed his thoughts concerning life after death in what are now classic words:

> I am standing upon the seashore. A ship at my side spreads her white sails to the morning breeze and starts for the blue ocean. She is an object of beauty and strength and I stand and watch until at last she hangs like a speck of white cloud just where the sea and sky come down to mingle with each other. Then someone at my side says, "There she goes!" Gone where? Gone from my sight . . . that is all. She is just as large in mast and hull and spar as she was when she left my side and just as able to bear her load of living freight to the place of destination. Her diminished size is in me, not in her. And just at the moment when someone at my side says, "There she goes," there are other eyes watching her coming and other voices ready to take up the glad shout, "There she comes!"

There is no question reflected in Jesus' ministry of his confidence that he would live beyond death. He sensed an intimate relationship with God, and the constant assumption throughout his ministry was that he would continue this relationship beyond the grave. Inasmuch as this belief was part of his basic understanding of himself and his followers, he never really argued the point. He never felt that this issue was something that he needed to prove, except when asked directly by the Sadducees. Things that are so obviously true to us do not need defense or argumentation. This seemed to be Jesus' feeling concerning life after death.

A less classical and more intimate expression was shared with me by an older colleague in ministry. In December, 1973, I wrote a brief note of condolence to Dr. W. Earle Smith, a retired executive minister of the San Francisco Bay Cities Baptist Union, upon the death of his wife. Shortly thereafter I received a response which included the following words:

> In my long life as a minister, I have only witnessed one soul passing from the body to meet the presence of the Eternal. That experience took place on December 9, 1973 when my beloved Lulu Wallace whispered in my ear that she loved me, and I saw her close her eyes and prepare to depart to meet her God. What a wonderful experience that was. As I watched her go, I realized that from the time when the Spirit of God had taken up His abode in her soul (92 years ago), that she had been the loving hostess to the eternal God throughout her long life and now she was going back to the giver of that life. It was an experience that I shall have only once in my life, and it was very real.

Judgment or Eternal Life?

As we turn specifically to Jesus' teachings concerning life after death, we find that they are both negative and positive. It may come as a surprise to us to find that Jesus has some negative teachings about the future. He did not avoid emphasis upon judgment and condemnation. We sometimes assume that Jesus came as a kindly, gracious teacher who never made any negative statements. The fact is, however, that there are no biblical statements concerning the coming judgment stronger than those that come from the lips of Jesus.

This teaching, concerning the coming judgment, is at once biblical and rational. As T. S. Eliot put it, "If we eliminate the doctrine of final judgment we convert God into Santa Claus—everybody shall get toys and be glad." The Christian understanding of the future is reflected in the Negro spiritual:

> God gave Noah the rainbow sign,
> No more water, the fire next time.

The announcement of coming judgment was not easy for Jesus or for the prophets, nor is it for the modern preacher. Soren Kierkegaard asked the question, "What happens to those who try to warn the present age?" He answered his own question with a brief parable:

> It happened that a fire broke out backstage in a theatre. The clown came out to inform the public. They thought he was just a jest and applauded. He repeated his warning, they shouted even louder. So I think the world will come to an end amid general applause from all the wits, who believe that it is a joke.[3]

When Jesus sent his followers as missionaries to the cities of Galilee, he expressed strong anticipation of future judgment. In the event that a city should reject one of his followers, he indicated that the disciple should wipe the dust off of his feet as a witness against the city. "I tell you, it shall be more tolerable on that day for Sodom than for that town" (Luke 10:12). Sodom, of course, was one of the cities that was destroyed in the time of Abraham. It was an evil city, and its destruction preceded the time of Jesus by centuries. Thus Jesus was speaking of future judgment when he spoke of Sodom being less under judgment than the city that would reject one of Jesus' followers.

Beyond this pronouncement, Jesus presented some strong teachings concerning hell. The English word "hell" primarily reflects two words in the original language of the New Testament. One word is the term "Hades" which simply meant the place where the dead go. The other word was "Gehenna."

Originally, Gehenna was a place outside the city of Jerusalem. On the western side of the ancient city was a valley which curved around the southern portion of the city called the Valley of Hinnon. Since the word for valley or earth was "Ge," the valley of Hinnon or "Ge Hinnon" became known as Gehenna.

In the Old Testament this valley was a place of evil. Some of the kings of Israel had worshiped foreign gods and had made human sacrifices in the valley. The good king Josiah polluted this territory because of its evil associations. In later days it was the city dump. A constant fire was said to burn in the valley in order to consume the garbage and the carcasses that were thrown there. This place became a picture of future judgment. When Jesus used the word "Gehenna" he used it figuratively. He was saying, "See the terrible valley outside the city? This is what the hell, the eternal Gehenna, will be like."

Jesus is commonly quoted by Matthew as speaking of this fiery hell to come. He says that some "shall be liable to the hell of fire" (Matthew 5:22); some will be "thrown into hell" (Matthew 5:29); and all evildoers will be thrown "into the furnace of fire; there men will weep and gnash their teeth" (Matthew 13:42). Sometimes Jesus referred not so much to the place of fire as to darkness. He called it the "outer darkness; there men will weep and gnash their teeth" (Matthew 22:13). Mark also quotes Jesus mentioning "the unquenchable fire" (Mark 9:44) and the hell "where their worm does not die, and the fire is not quenched" (Mark 9:48). Luke quotes Jesus referring to " 'this place of torment' " (Luke 16:28). It is obvious, then, that Jesus used severe language to describe the ultimate fate of those who are impenitent before God. The strongest language concerning hell to be found in the New Testament came from the lips of Jesus.

"This means that a person who chooses to walk in darkness will in the great future find himself in the outer darkness," says Dutch theologian Hendrikus Berkhof. "Hell is the consequences of God's respect for our humanity." So is heaven.

As C. S. Lewis once depicted it in a play, it is when God, after beseeching a person's friendship throughout earthly life, at last agrees, "Thy will be done."

At Southampton's fashionable St. Andrew's Dune Church, after a week of steaming hot weather, the Reverend William Henry Wagner told the congregation he would preach the shortest sermon ever. It consisted of the following words: "If you think it's hot here—just *wait!*"

It is probably unnecessary to point out that Jesus spoke in more positive terms with reference to life after death. This was the purpose of his coming, according to the New Testament. We should note, however, that his words concerning the kingdom or eternal life did not simply relate to an endless existence. Some have assumed that eternal life is an endless extension of the kind of existence that we now know. On the contrary, the sense of eternal life as taught by Jesus is rooted in character. It relates to a quality of life.

There is a genuine change in us as we come to relate to God through Jesus Christ. This change is the beginning of eternal life here and now. The life that comes after death is simply an extension of this new quality of existence. Thus it is the quality, as well as the quantity, of life that is important when we speak of eternity.

This fact becomes most clear, of course, in John's Gospel. Again and again Jesus spoke about eternal life as something into which we have already entered. Jesus said, ". . . he who hears my word and believes him who sent me, *has* eternal life" (John 5:24, author's emphasis). This life is in the present tense. We already have it. Nevertheless, it does relate to the future. We shall be delivered from judgment and brought into an extension of this new quality of life. Thus Jesus indicates that the believer "does not come into judgment, but has passed from death to life" (John 5:24).

When Robert Browning died, Sir Edward Burne–Jones came away from the depressing funeral service, saying, "I would have given something for a banner or two, and much more would I have given if a chorister had come out from the triforium and rent the air with a trumpet!"

Browning was the kind of person of whom Teilhard de Chardin spoke in saying, "The world will belong tomorrow to those who gave it hope today." Such hope is given by those who have hope. Henri Nouwen has said,

A man or a woman without hope in the future cannot live creatively in the present. The paradox of expectation indeed is that those who believe in tomorrow can better live today. That those who expect joy to come out of sadness can discover the beginning of new life.

Such hope is also reflected in a passage of Paul Tournier:

It is he also who then becomes our reason for hoping. "I remember," writes Dr. Sebillotte, "an old woman whose faith in Jesus as Saviour was quite solid. She suffered a cerebral hemorrhage and realized that she could not recover. Almost her last words were: 'At last I'm going to know.' The doctor goes on: 'Those who saw her there lying dead that Easter morning, as she had wished, also wait to know.' "

That same remark, "I'm going to know," was said to me, word for word, during a recent visit. It was to one of my former patients, an old lady of more than ninety now, more or less housebound. She had written to say that she wished to see me again. It was a wonderful conversation, for there is a strong spiritual bond between us. We talked about death. I had known her as a scrupulous soul, inclined to worry. I found her at peace, and serene. She said: "I am ready to go on living, and I am ready to die. At last, I am going to know." The next day she wrote me a letter, as if to prolong our meeting: "for myself," she wrote, "I shall be very happy to see that beyond, and perhaps to hear Christ himself talking about the mysteries of the grace of God."[4]

The primary emphasis of the New Testament concerning Jesus' resurrection is the fact that he *is* risen. Remarkably little is said about the specific act of his rising from the dead. The New Testament rather deals with the witness of the many who knew our Lord in his continuing risen state. The emphasis is upon the "now." For the modern Christian to believe truly in the resurrection is to know the presence of Christ in daily life. Lewis Carroll's *Through the Looking Glass* points up the importance of the present in the denial of today by the Queen who was "living backwards":

> ". . . and I don't care for jam."
> "It's very good jam," said the Queen.
> "Well, I don't want any *today*, at any rate."
> "You couldn't have it if you *did* want it," the Queen said. "The rule is, jam to-morrow and jam yesterday—but never jam *today.*"
> "It *must* come sometimes to 'jam today,' " Alice objected.
> "No, it can't," said the Queen. "It's jam every *other* day: today isn't any *other* day, you know."[5]

Gerald O'Collins has observed the fact that numerous theologians have resembled the Queen in laying down "the rule" that there was resurrection yesterday (Christ's); there will be resurrection tomorrow (the general resurrection at the end); but there is never resurrection today.[6]

Elisabeth Kubler–Ross witnesses to the importance of the now. "For me, Easter is a personal, daily encounter with the healing, enlivening, transforming power of the Spirit making me know, beyond the shadow of a doubt, that there is life after death—and it is for this that I am being readied."[7]

We may now ask how the life to come is determined. What is the deciding factor as to whether this life will be negative or positive? The answer to this question is probably best reflected in Jesus' statement concerning himself as an advocate for his followers. "So every one who acknowledges me before men, I also will acknowledge before my Father who is in heaven; but whoever denies me before men, I also will deny before my Father who is in heaven" (Matthew 10:32, 33). Thus Jesus is indicating that he who himself has exemplified God's love and grace among us will also serve as the advocate who will determine God's judgment. His witness before God as to our response or denial will be the determining factor with reference to the life to come. Will I enter into eternal life or into judgment? The answer is determined completely by my response to Jesus Christ. He will be the judge.

It remains to be asked when we shall enter into this life after death. Is it immediately after death or at some future judgment of God? Jesus does teach of the coming great day of judgment. He implies that we move into the presence of God immediately upon dying, though this teaching is not explicit.

R. William Herzog, of the American Baptist Seminary of the West, describes an experience of pastoral relationship:

> While pastoring a small church, I was asked to visit a widow whose husband had died a few months before I was called to the parish. We spent a most important afternoon discussing her loss and how she was coping with it. As I was leaving, she took my hand, looked me in the eye, and asked quite intently, "Pastor where is my husband now?" Caught off guard, I responded, "I don't know but I can tell you something more important than that. I can tell you in whose hands he is."
>
> She responded with remarkable candor, "Thank you. I wouldn't have believed you if you had given me a pat answer, and what you

have said gives me more than enough comfort."[8]

You may remember that Jesus told a story about a rich man and a poor man who had died. Both went into the life to come upon the point of their death. You will, likely, also remember Jesus' words to the thief who was beside him on the cross. He said, "Truly, I say to you, *today* you will be with me in Paradise" (Luke 23:43, author's emphasis). Jesus seems to teach that we enter into a place of joy and relationship with God immediately upon death.

When Dr. W. E. Sangster lay dying with muscular atrophy, he wrote to Billy Graham. Among other things, he said,

All my life I have preached that Jesus Christ is adequate for every crisis. I have but a few days to live, and oh, Billy, Christ is indeed adequate in the hour of death. Tell everyone it is true. Tell them from me that God is wonderfully near his children as they come to the end of life's road.

In conclusion we may summarize what Jesus teaches about life after death. He taught that we would be raised either to judgment or eternal life. The determination of this negative or positive relationship to God will be through our response and relationship with God through Christ in this life. There are many questions that are left to us, but these broad outlines are clear. It is not for us to guess and speculate. It is for us to respond and relate to God through the grace of our Lord Jesus Christ. This is the beginning of life eternal—to know God and Jesus Christ whom God has sent.

> I will repudiate the lie
> Men tell of life:
> How it will pass
> As fragile flower, or butterfly,
> Whose dust shall nourish
> April grass.
> Since One, for love, died on a tree
> and in the stony
> Tomb has lain,
> Behold I show a mystery:
> All sepulchres
> Are sealed in vain![9]
> —John Richard Moreland

Notes

Preface

1. Janet Whitney, *John Woolman: American Quaker.* (Boston: Little, Brown and Company, 1942), pp. 305-309.

Chapter 1

1. Edward LeLoly, *Mother Theresa of Calcutta.* (San Francisco: Harper & Row, 1983), p. 44. Quoted in *Newsweek* (10/29/79), p. 60.

2. Two Hebrew words are translated "man" in Psalm 8:4. Neither refers to male gender. *Enosh* describes humanity and is rarely used of individuals, much less of a specific male. It probably derives from the verb *anash,* "to be weak, sick," referring to our human fraility as mortal, earthly beings, not to our gender. *Adam,* similarly referring to humankind both male and female (Genesis 5:2), takes both plural pronouns (Genesis 1:26) and plural verb forms (Genesis 1:27). See Phyllis Trible, *God and the Rhetoric of Sexuality* (Philadelphia: Fortress Press, 1978), p. 18.

3. Irving Stone, *Love Is Eternal.* (Garden City, New York: Doubleday & Company, Inc., 1954), p. 234.

4. David M. Paton, ed., *Breaking Barriers: Nairobi 1975.* The Official Report of the Fifth Assembly of the World Council of Churches, Nairobi, 23 November-10 December, 1975. (Grand Rapids: William B. Eerdmans, 1976). Pages 23-24 contain a summary of Professor Birch's address. The full text is in the library of the Ecumenical Centre of the World Council of Churches, Geneva, Switzerland.

5. Robert L. Short, *The Gospel According to Peanuts.* (Richmond, Virginia: John Knox Press, 1964), p.46.

6. William Temple, *Readings in St. John's Gospel.* (London: Macmillan and Co., Limited, 1939), p.24.

7. Paul Tillich, *The Shaking of the Foundations.* (New York: Charles Scribners Sons, 1948), p.162.

Chapter 2

1. J. B. Phillips, *Your God Is Too Small.* (New York: Macmillan Publishing Company, 1954), pp. 9-63.

2. R. A. Knox, *The Belief of Catholics.* (New York: Sheed and Ward, 1940), chap. IV. R. A. Knox, *Some Loose Stones.* (London: Longmans, Green and Company, 1913), chap. III.

3. James Weldon Johnson, "The Creation," *God's Trombones.* Quoted from *The Book of Negro Poetry.* (New York: Harcourt, Brace and World, Inc., 1958), p. 117.

4. A. J. Cronin, *Adventures in Two Worlds.* (New York: McGraw-Hill Book Company, 1935), p. 323.

5. Cronin, pp. 172-180.

6. Martin Luther King, Jr., a Ph. D. dissertation: "A Comparison of the Conceptions of God in the Thinking of Paul Tillich and Henry Nelson Weiman." (Boston University, 1955), p. 275.

7. C. S. Lewis, *The Joyful Christian.* (New York: Macmillan Publishing Company Inc., 1977), p. 38.

8. Lewis, p. 35.

9. Letha Scanzoni and Nancy Hardesty, *All We're Meant to Be.* (Waco, Texas: Word Inc., 1974), p. 20.

10. Frederick Buechner, *The Magnificent Defeat.* (New York: Seabury Press, 1966), p. 47.

11. Robert McCracken, *Questions People Ask.* (New York: Harper and Brothers, 1951), p. 67.

12. John Hick, *Christianity at the Centre.* (New York: Herder and Herder, 1970), p. 42.

13. H. E. Scudder, ed., "The Eternal Goodness," *The Poetical Works of Whittier,* Cambridge Edition. (Boston: Houghton Mifflin Company, 1975), p. 442.

Chapter 3

1. Mary Livingston Benny and Hilliard Marks with Marcia Borie, *Jack Benny.* (New York: Doubleday & Company, Inc., 1978), p. 303.

2. Soren Kierkegaard, *Work of Love.* (New York: Harper and Brothers, 1962), pp. 92, 95.

3. C. S. Lewis, *Mere Christianity.* (New York: Macmillan Publishing Company, 1958), p. 101.

4. Helmut Thielicke, *Our Heavenly Father.* (New York: Harper & Row, Publishing Inc., 1960), p. 93.

5. Lewis, pp. 90-91.

6. C. G. Jung, *Psychology and Religion: West and East,* Volume 11, Bollingen Series XX, The Collected Works of C. G. Jung. (Princeton: Princeton University Press, 2nd Edition, 1969), p. 339.

7. Anders Nygren, *Agape and Eros.* (Philadelphia: The Westminster Press, 1953.)

8. Similar verse concerning various theologians is presented by Hugh T. Kerr, "Not Like They Used To," *Theology Today,* vol. XXXII, no. 1 (April, 1975), pp. 1-6.

9. Helmut Thielicke, *Christ and the Meaning of Life.* (New York: Harper and Brothers, 1962), pp. 112-113.

10. *The Teaching of the Twelve Apostles Commonly Called the Didache* in The Library of Christian Classics, vol. I, Early Christian Fathers. (Philadelphia: The Westminster Press, 1953), p.171.

11. Lewis, p. 90.

12. Helmut Thielicke, *Christ and the Meaning of Life.* (New York: Harper and Brothers, 1962), p. 113.

13. Johnathan Messerli, *Horace Mann: A Biography.* (New York: Alfred A. Knopf, 1972), p. 225.

14. Gene Bartlett, *The Authentic Pastor.* (Valley Forge: Judson Press, 1978), pp. 59-60.

15. Harry Emerson Fosdick, *Twelve Tests of Character.* (New York: Association Press, 1923), pp. 166-167.

Chapter 4

1. George Burns, *The Third Time Around.* (New York: G. P. Putnam's Sons, 1980), p. 199.

2. Frederick B. Speakman, *The Salty Tang.* (Westwood, New Jersey: Fleming H. Revel Company, 1954), p. 97.

Chapter 5

1. Seneca, *De Benefices,* iii. 16.2; Juvenal, *Satires,* vi. 24; Demosthenes, *Orations,* vii. 41.

2. Herbert Danby, *The Mishnah.* (London: Oxford University Press, 1933), p. 321.

3. Matthew Henry, *Commentary on the Whole Bible.* Edited by Leslie F. Church. (Grand Rapids: Zondervan Publishing House, 1960), p. 7.

4 Paul Tournier, *Guilt and Grace: A Psychological Study.* (London: Hodder & Stoughton, 1962), pp. 124-125.

Chapter 6

1. Richard Ostling, "This Is a God I Can Trust," *Time,* vol. 116, no. 26 (December 29, 1980), p. 67.

2. F. F. Bruce, *The Letters of Paul: An Expanded Paraphrase.* (Grand Rapids: William B. Eerdmans Company, 1965), p. 249.

3. C. S. Lewis, *The Joyful Christian.* (New York: Macmillan Publishing Company, 1977), p. 51.

4. Charles F. D. Moule, *The Birth of the New Testament.* (London: Adam and Charles Black, 1962), p. 9.

5. Oscar Cullman, *The Christology of the New Testament.* (Philadelphia: The Westminster Press, 1959.)

6. Gene Bartlett, *The Authentic Pastor.* (Valley Forge: Judson Press, 1978), p. 106.

7. C. S. Lewis, *Mere Christianity.* (London & Glasgow: Collins, Fontana Books, 1955), p. 52.

Chapter 7

1. Edith Lovejoy Pierce, "On the Shooting of Archbishop Romero," *Christian Century,* vol. XCVII, no. 14 (April 16, 1980), p. 437.

2. Elisabeth Kubler-Ross, *On Death and Dying.* (New York: Macmillan Publishing Company, 1969.)

3. W. Somerset Maugham, *The Moon and Sixpence, The Modern Library* (New York: Doubleday & Company, Inc.), p. 97. Used by permission.

4. Rollo May, *The Art of Counseling.* (New York, Abingdon-Cokesbury Press, 1939), p. 159.

5. Dorothy Berkely Phillips, ed., *The Choice Is Always Ours.* (New York: Harper & Row, Publishers Inc., 1960), p. 67.

6. Edwin Markham, "Victory in Defeat," *Masterpieces of Religious Verse.* Edited by James Dalton Morrison. (New York: Harper and Brothers, 1948), p. 292.

7. Hosius, "Letter Apud Opera," 112–113, *Baptist Magazine,* vol. CVIII (May, 1826), p. 278.

8. Frank S. Mead, *See These Banners Go.* (New York: The Bobbs-Merrill Company, 1934), p. 131.

Chapter 8

1. Gene Barlett, *The Authentic Pastor.* (Valley Forge: Judson Press), p. 19.

2. Alfred Lord Tennyson, *Idylls of the King: The Story of King Arthur and His Court.* (New York: The Heritage Press, 1939), p. 285.

Chapter 9

1. Wolfgang Roth and Rosemary Radford Ruether, *The Liberating Bond: Covenants—Biblical and Contemporary.* (New York: Friendship Press, 1978), p. 12.

2. Bernard Ramm, *After Fundamentalism: The Future of Evangelical Theology.* (San Francisco: Harper & Row, Publishers Inc., 1983), pp. 187-188.

3. F. F. Bruce, *Paul: Apostle of the Heart Set Free.* (Grand Rapids: William B. Eerdmans Publishing Company, 1977), p. 463.

4. Soren Kierkegaard, *Works of Love.* (New York: Harper and Brothers, 1962), p. 294.

5. Bruce, p. 461.

Chapter 10

1. George Bernard Shaw, *Pygmalion and Other Plays.* (New York: Dodd, Mead & Company 1967), p. 99.

2. F. F. Bruce, *Paul: Apostle of the Heart Set Free.* (Grand Rapids: William B. Eerdmans Publishing Company, 1977), p. 99.

3. Elton Trueblood, *Alternative to Futility.* (New York: Harper and Brothers, 1948), pp. 38-39.

Chapter 11

1. John Donne, *Devotions Upon Emergent Occasions.* (Ann Arbor: The University of Michigan Press, 1978), pp. 108-109.

2. E. Stanley Jones, *The Unshakable Kingdom and the Unchanging Person.* (Nashville: Abingdon Press, 1972), p. 40.

3. Walter E. Woodbury, "Evangelism: The American Baptist Home Mission Society Annual Report of the Board," *Annual of the Northern Baptist Convention.* (Philadelphia: American Baptist Publication Society, 1937), p. 637.

4. Edward LeLoly, *Mother Teresa of Calcutta.* (San Franciso: Harper & Row, Publishers Inc., 1983), p. 162.

5. Bernard Ramm, *After Fundamentalism: The Future of Evangelical Theology.* (San Francisco: Harper & Row, Publishers Inc., 1983), p. 150.

6. Harry Fleischman, *Let's Be Human.* (July-August, 1984.)

7. Keith Miller, *Habitation of Dragons.* (Waco, Texas: Word Books, 1970), p. 51.

8. "Pudd'nhead Wilson's New Calendar, Introducing Mark Twain," *Following the Equator,* vol. II, chap. III. (New York: Harper and Brothers, 1897), p. 35.

9. Elton Trueblood, *Alternative to Futility.* (New York: Harper and Brothers, 1948), p. 39.

10. J. S. Whale, *Christian Doctrine.* (Cambridge: The University Press, 1956), pp. 145-146.

Chapter 12

1. Martin Buber, *Tales of the Hasidim,* vol. 1, *The Early Masters,* and vol. 2, *The Later Masters.* (New York: Schocken Books, 1947).

2. Thomas W. Gillespie, "The Ministry of God," *Princeton Seminary Bulletin,* vol V, no. 1 (February, 1984), p.1.

3. Edna St. Vincent Millay, "To Jesus on His Birthday," *Masterpieces of Religious Verse.* Edited by James Dalton Morrison. (New York: Harper and Brothers, 1948), p. 168.

4. Ron Reid, "On the Spirit of Joy and Some Joy of the Spirit," *Sports Illustrated,* vol. 46, no. 10 (February 28, 1977), p. 37.

5. Ernest Best, *From Text to Sermon.* (Atlanta: John Knox Press, 1978), p. 54.

6. Sancti Avrelli Avgvstine, *Quaestianes Evangeliorum,* II, 19. Warren S. Kissinger, *The Parables of Jesus.* (London: The Scarecrow Press, Inc., 1979), pp. 26-27.

7. Thomas C. Oden, *Parables of Kierkegaard.* (Princeton: Princeton University Press, 1978), pp. xiii-xiv.

8. Malcolm Muggeridge, *Jesus Rediscovered.* (Garden City, New York: Doubleday & Company, Inc., 1969), p. 79.

Chapter 13

1. Paul Tournier, *Learn to Grow Old.* (New York, Harper & Row, 1971), p. 218.

2. Dorothy Gilman, *A New Kind of Country.* (Garden City, New York: Doubleday & Company, Inc., 1978), p. 106.

3. Soren Kierkegaard, *Either/Or: A Fragment of Life,* vol. I, translated by Daniel F. Swenson and Lillian Marvin Swenson. (Princeton: Princeton University Press, 1949), p. 24.

4. Tournier, pp. 240-241.

5. Lewis Carroll, *Through the Looking Glass.* (New York: Random House, 1946), p. 72.

6. Gerald O'Collins, *What Are They Saying About the Resurrection?* (New York: Paulist Press, 1978), pp. 22-24.

7. Elisabeth Kubler-Ross, "Letters," *The Christian Century.* (July 21–28, 1976), p. 670.

8. William R. Herzog, II, "Teaching–Learning Resources," *Baptist Leader,* vol. 45, no. 8 (November, 1984), p. 48.

9. John Richard Moreland, "If a Man Die Shall He Live Again?" from "A Blue Wave Breaking," *Masterpieces of Religious Verse.* Edited by James Dalton Morrison. (New York: Harper and Brothers, 1948), p. 604.